MW01256683

Out of the Shadows

Out of the Shadows:
Exploring the many facets of gambling and their implications to society

Edward H. Sodergren, Ph.D.

Mill City Press, Inc.

FOREWARD

Gambling has recently been referred to as the "fastest growth industry in the world." And, at the same time, it is being called "America's latest social addiction."

During the course of history, gambling has been alternatively labeled as a sin, a vice, a deviant behavior, a moral weakness, entertainment, and even a civic responsibility.

It has changed lives. It has brought untold wealth to some, yet sorrow and even death to others.

How does this happen? How is it that there can be so many varied responses to this one single activity?

This book was written in the hope that it could shed some light on gambling as we know it today.

It was written with the primary intent to serve as a resource for those persons in the helping professions who have had little or no exposure to the activity, its potential for problems, or the possibility of treatment for what is currently referred to as the "hidden disease."

Additionally, the information contained herein is presented in such a way as to allow the lay reader a comprehensive appreciation of the subject matter as well.

The reader will become familiar with the history of gambling, its evolution, growth, prevalence, participants, and potential for problems, as well as recommended treatment responses. And, hopefully, the many facets that comprise the enigma we know as gambling will be brought Out of the Shadows.

CONTENTS

CHAPTER ONE

Introduction

Statement of the Problem

"Since the beginning of civilization, large numbers of people have been willing to risk their money on the outcome of some unpredictable event" (Shaffer, 1993, p. 4), the activity that we know today as gambling.

McGurrin (1992) discusses the finds of artifacts as well as documentation by archeologists that establish for certain the fact that human beings have wagered on the outcome of chance events for at least the past 6,000 years. And, there is some disagreement among theorists as to the origins of this wagering. Some believe that it derives from the occult aspects of early religion and its efforts to foretell the future, whereas others think it was used by politicians and monarchs to distract people from the discomfort of experiencing food shortages or some other social calamity. And yet another group regarded this activity as simply a function of natural play and recreation.

It is also documented that, whatever the origins and role this activity had in society, it brought with it the problem, for some, of engaging in it uncontrollably. In Shaffer (1993) there is reference to attempts by governments to control gambling activity as early as 300 B.C.

The Babylonians, the Etruscans, and ancient Chinese civilizations were participants in organized gambling (McGurrin, 1992). The Bible mentions casting lots, a form of gambling, and tells of Roman soldiers gambling with dice, contesting for the garments of Christ at his crucifixion.

In Shaffer's (1992) references to the history of gambling, he refers not only to the activity of gambling but to its apparent problems and attempts to control it even then. He states that during the Third Crusade in A.D. 1190, Richard the Lionhearted issued orders restricting dice playing among his troops. His knights and clergymen were limited to a maximum of 20 shillings in losses, but ordinary soldiers were not allowed to participate in gambling at all. This policy appeared to suggest that some individuals could control their gambling while others could not. Shaffer sees this as an early lay theory that perhaps certain personal characteristics predisposed some individuals to loss of control.

Shaffer further reports that it was thought that only the lower classes were affected by gambling problems. However, a significant incident in the sixteenth century tended to dispute this belief. While gambling with his noblemen, King Henry VIII lost the Jesus bells that hung from the tower of St. Paul's Cathedral. This incident provided evidence that gambling problems permeated all social strata.

To further emphasize the historical existence of gambling problems Rosenthal (1992) tells of the origin of pathological gamblers being known as addicts.

The *Oxford English Dictionary* refers to addiction as enslavement, and to its first English usage as the enslavement of one person to another.

The Latin origins of the word *addict* are described as the prefix *ad*, meaning "in the direction of" or "toward," and the root of the word, *dict*, which is the same as in dictate and diction, meaning "to speak."

In early Roman times most people were illiterate, so the emphasis was on the spoken law. At this time of rampant gambling the original addict was someone who could not pay his gambling debts, resulting in his being brought into court where the judge verbally addressed the terms of the individual's punishment, sentencing the accused into slavery.

In more recent times in America, prior to the mass arrival of Europeans, gambling was a part of the culture of the Native American tribes. The Iroquois played with dice made from peach pits, and the Narraganset played dice games with all members of the tribe participating. Although a social activity, observers reported that, while some participants controlled their gambling, others exhibited more compulsive and excessive behaviors (Shaffer 1992).

McGurrin (1992) describes the history of gambling in early America as being integral from Colonial times. Early Americans bet on horse racing, dog and cock fights, and lotteries even though the activity of gambling was considered a moral vice. This immoral and sinful perception of gambling was embraced and perpetuated by the American judicial process as each of the original 13 states incorporated English anti-gambling laws.

This did little to dissuade the general public from its gambling behavior. In fact, the popularity of gambling, combined with the financial need of the government, led to the development of public lotteries as a way of financing construction of roads, bridges, fortifications, schools, hospitals, and even churches. These lotteries were very popular and flourished in spite of the illegal status of gambling.

Little changed in the 19th century, during which time the activity of gambling maintained its popular status even as the laws against it intensified.

Continuing on, McGurrin describes the activities of the 20th century and the widespread public rejection of the legal prohibition of gambling, beginning in 1931 when the State of Nevada legalized most forms of gambling, including casino gambling. The 1940s saw the legalization of parimutuel horse racing along the Eastern Seaboard and in some Midwestern states. Circumstances remained this way until 1964 when New Hampshire began the first modern-day legal lottery. This began a new wave of legalized gambling. By 1984, 22 states had authorized lotteries. New York and Connecticut offered government-operated off-track betting, and New Jersey legalized casino gambling in Atlantic City. In 1989 the State Legislature of Iowa approved riverboat gambling along the Mississippi River, continuing the growth of opportunity to gamble.

The move in Iowa was a definite change in policy in that, 17 years earlier, in 1972, a Catholic priest had been arrested in Dubuque, Iowa for sponsoring a church sanctioned bingo game (*The Economist U.S.* December 13, 1997).

Also, during the last two decades there has been a birth and growth of gambling opportunities offered by Native American Indians. The Indian gambling movement began with a 1987 United States Supreme Court decision stating that the Cabazon Band of Mission Indians of Riverside County, California, should be allowed to offer public bingo. This decision then led to Congress passing the Indian Gaming Regulatory Act of 1998, which states that because of the sovereign status of the Indians, they could offer the same type of gambling that the State allowed anyone else (Dickey, 2000).

Historically, as the activity of gambling grew, the public perception of the activity correspondingly went through a process of change. As reported by Rose (1993), the activity of gambling 200 years ago was considered a sin. In the 18th century the word "gamble" was a term of reproach while "gambler" originally meant a fraudulent gamester. Gambling was viewed as unholy, the gambler was overtly condemned, and the excessive gambler was destined for Hell.

The 19th century saw a change in the perception of gambling from not so much a sin as a vice. The gambler was seen as weak, and the view was that those who gave in to the vice were deserving of whatever misfortune they received.

Finally, the 20th century, 1980 to be exact, saw the inclusion of pathological gambling in the American Psychiatric Association's *Diagnostic and Statistical Manual of Mental Disorders* (DSM-III). This position now challenged the idea that anyone who gambles problematically does so of his own free will.

However, this progression from sin to vice to disease has not been embraced by everyone. The current perception of pathological gambling has been called, by some, "the hidden disease," because of a lack of laboratory findings or any direct physical associations, such as needle marks, an odor, or observable changes of behavior. But this disorder is still viewed by others in moralistic terms in which they view gambling as a sign of social evil, a carnal vice, or simply a case of deteriorated personal values (Miller, 1996).

Regardless of opinion, gambling plays a very significant role in today's society.

In 1974 the number of Americans who gambled was 61 percent of the total population. They legally wagered $17.4 billion. In 1989 the Gallup organization reported that 71 percent of the American public gambled, while the gross legal gaming dollar amount handled was $246.9 billion for the year. Although these figures reflect only a 10 percent increase of the total population as far as the number of persons gambling, it is of significant note that the dollar volume increased 1,400 percent in those 15 years (Lesieur, 1992).

These figures are further supported by Berman and Seigel (1992), who reported that in 1992 gambling was a $300 billion-a-year industry and was growing at a rate of 10 percent annually. That would make the 1999 dollar amount wagered legally in the United States approximately $600 billion.

As the numbers of Americans gambling increased from 61 percent in the 1970s to 71 percent in the 1980s to 80 percent in the 1990s, correspondingly the rates of related gambling problems within this population grew as well – from 0.77 percent in 1974 to 1.4 percent in 1984 to 3.4 percent in 1988 (Viets and Miller, 1997).

A December 13, 1997, article in *The Economist U.S.* (page 22) cites a report by Harvard Medical School stating that the number of Americans with severe gambling disorders has increased by 55 percent over the past two decades.

As opportunities to gamble grow, so apparently do its problems. And further research in this area shows that the ability of our current system to respond to these problems is lacking. Only about 1 percent or less of the people with compulsive gambling problems receive help for their problem (Estes and Brubaker, 1994).

Currently, there are fewer than 12 inpatient treatment facilities and 100 outpatient programs in the whole of the United States that are treating those people experiencing gambling problems (Burke, 1996).

In the findings of Estes and Brubaker (1994), they refer frequently to information provided to them by Dr. Durand Jacobs, Clinical Professor of Psychiatry at Loma Linda University Medical School, Loma Linda, California, and former Program Director of the Compulsive Gambling Treatment Program at the Veterans Administration Hospital in Loma Linda, California, now retired.

They report that Dr. Jacobs' position is that compulsive gambling is the last of the major addictions to be addressed in this country. They say that Dr. Jacobs believes that the public is well aware of the problems of alcohol, drugs, smoking, and overeating, and that some sort of professional assistance is readily available for all these disorders, but that is not the case with gambling. With gambling, there is a tremendous shortage of treatment resources. Also, Dr. Jacobs believes that only a handful of clinicians in the United States are skilled in the diagnosis and treatment of compulsive gambling and that, to his knowledge, no physician, no psychiatrist, no psychologist, no social worker, nor any marriage and family counselors have ever received any formal graduate training in compulsive gambling treatment. Instead, he believes that everything learned thus far regarding this disorder has been as a result of trial and error.

In a study by Miller (1996), he supports Jacobs' position regarding lack of treatment resources in the United States. He reports that by the end of the 1980s there were only 50 private-sector specialty clinics and treatment centers for pathological gambling in all of the United States. Because of this, he supports brief intervention treatment modalities by qualified caregivers. The problem, in his view, is that there are not many clinicians who have a developed expertise in the diagnosis and treatment of pathological gambling.

Further research indicates support of this problem. *The Harvard Mental Health Letter* (January 1996, p. 3) reports that mental health professionals do not always look for, or indeed recognize, the problem of pathological gambling when presented with it.

In an article by Franklin and Ciarrocchi (1987), they report that it is not at all surprising that there is a problem in developing professional competence to treat pathological gambling problems, due to the scarcity of available treatment resources.

Volberg and Steadman (1992) report that, even with the magnitude of the growth of gambling and the generation of increased revenues for individual state governments, funds for treatment are being greatly reduced or, in some cases, eliminated. The reason for this is an under-utilization of current programs, not due to a lack of need, but rather a poorly focused effort in identification of the problem.

Gambling in some form is currently legal in 48 of the 50 United States, the exceptions being Utah and Hawaii, with 27 states having legalized casino gambling (Pasternak, 1997).

To further avail the American public of opportunities to gamble, the last decade has seen the birth and rapid growth of casino type gambling on lands owned by Native Americans. There are currently approximately 554 different Native American tribes in the United States. Of these, 100 tribes operate 200 casinos in 28 states with more coming into existence annually (Gold and Ferrel, 1998).

Cited research would appear to indicate a continued period of growth of opportunities for gambling, with additional numbers of individuals negatively affected and a system lacking the ability to identify and treat those problems. The proliferation of opportunities to gamble is, in and of itself, not a problem for those who are able to gamble. However, these opportunities will allow greater access to and, subsequently, promote development and growth of problems among those who are susceptible.

In Viets and Miller (1997), they state that "as the number of legally sanctioned casinos, lotteries, and other gambling opportunities increase, pathological gambling is likely to become a widespread problem" (p. 689).

So, based on the preceding research findings, the problem appears to be multifaceted. There has recently been, and continues to be, a growth of opportunities to gamble, which in turn appears to result in an increase in the number of individuals being negatively affected by fallout problems. In combination with the lack of any significant increase in the availability of treatment considerations, as well as the fact that this "hidden disease" remains an enigma to many health care professionals, it would appear that we have what Mobilia (1993) describes as "gambling, America's latest social addiction" (p. 122).

These concerns, then, have become the majority contributors to the purpose of this book, as an attempt is made to answer the question: "Based on current theory and research, what components should be included in the identification and treatment of problem gambling?"

Statement of Purpose

"In the hands of an experienced therapist, pathological gambling is an extremely treatable disorder." (Rosenthal, 1992, p. 5).

As true as this statement may be, research findings as presented in the "Statement of Problem" chapter of this book have indicated that the activity of gambling will continue to grow, the associative problems will increase, and the treatment personnel and facilities will remain limited.

And so, if pathological gambling is an extremely treatable disorder, as Rosenthal implies, but yet this problem is going unaddressed due to a lack of treatment resources, the problem presented is how to increase treatment resource availability. The purpose of this book is to explore current research and theory in an attempt to answer this question: What are the necessary considerations for helping professionals who treat clients with pathological gambling disorders?

By examining and reporting on current research findings, information is provided to allow for a greater understanding of the activity of gambling and the dynamics surrounding the problems that it may produce.

In Moran (1993, p. 138) he asks:

How can psychologists and other professionals make sense of this situation in a more rational manner? It seems to me that the only way that we can do this is to recognize that gambling behavior is a continuum from total abstinence to occasional gambling and from there to moderate gambling and finally to heavy gambling, which ultimately leads to problems.

This book provides information addressing itself to the complete continuum presented by Moran with its greatest emphasis focusing on the final stage of that continuum, the problem.

The problem area itself is one of complexity. Taber (1987, p. 221) states:

Problem, excessive, and pathological gambling can be conceptualized in terms of addictionology, biology, genetics, disease process, values clarification, forensic responsibility, learning failure, developmental disorder, anthropological matrix, social dynamic, impulse control, economic man, political resource theory, and, yes, in terms of statistical learning theory and schedules of reinforcement.

He goes on to say:
> To invest in any single formula would constitute irrational longshot gambling on our part since, no matter how useful and internally consistent any single model may be, none yet presented comes anywhere close to covering all human risk taking situations (p. 220).

Based on the position presented by Taber, this book addresses a number of proposed contributors to the problem of pathological gambling.

McGurrin (1992) supports the position espoused by Taber and states that:
> Although gambling is an ancient and universal human activity, recognition of a psychopathological manifestation of gambling and efforts to reliably diagnose and effectively treat this psychosocial disorder have existed since only about 1970. Consequently, the research and treatment techniques used in dealing with pathological gambling are tentative and incomplete. Much has been borrowed from the field of addictions and substance abuse because of fundamental and recurrent similarities between pathological gambling and addictive disorders.
>
> The shared treatment techniques also are justified on the basis of the rather high percentage of multiple or cross addictions found among pathological gamblers and substance abusers. Nevertheless, there are also many researchers and practitioners who object to adoption of the addictions model in understanding and treating pathological gambling.
>
> The knowledge and treatment of pathological gambling will be modified many times before it stabilizes on a well-tested scientific foundation.
>
> The practitioner, therefore, must provide treatment now based on the best knowledge available (p. IX).

This, then, becomes the purpose of this book: to attempt to provide knowledge to health care professionals currently in a position to help those individuals suffering from this disorder of pathological gambling, by increasing their levels of awareness as they attempt to identify, diagnose, refer, and/or treat as circumstances and abilities dictate and allow.

Definition of Terms

In recent years the activity of gambling has developed as a significant subculture within our society. Resulting from this group has been the introduction of a new lexicon, specific not only to gamblers, but also to those persons involved in associated activities, up to and including treatment professionals.

Following are a number of words and phrases from this new language, defined for the readers of this book in the hope of providing them with a more comprehensive grasp of this issue.

Action: the activity of gambling, playing the games, and making the bets, resulting in an aroused or euphoric state similar to that of a high from a drug.

Action gambler: competitive; prefers cards, dice, racing, and stock market as games of choice; perceives himself as skillful and gambles for a feeling of power.

Addiction: dependence characterized by chronicity, compulsiveness, and uncontrollable urges to use a substance or to perform an activity; the attempt to cut down on, control, or stop the activity or use causes severe emotional, mental, and/or psychological reactions.

Antisocial Personality Gambler: when losing and needing to stay in the action, may turn to illegal activities for money; however, unlike a true antisocial personality, the gambler feels guilt and remorse about these actions, rationalizes his inappropriate behavior, and fully intends to make restitution when his luck changes.

Bailout: when the gambler turns to others, usually family, with a request for financial help to escape a desperate situation caused by gambling (perhaps the writing of bad checks, embezzlement, etc.). This request for financial assistance is usually accompanied by the gambler's promise to stop gambling.

Casual Social Gambler: gambles for recreation and excitement. Although winning is the primary objective, when losing occurs, the losses are considered the cost of the entertainment. This type of gambling has no negative impact on family, social, or vocational obligations, and the gambler is in control.

Chasing: the continuation of gambling with previously non-allocated resources of time and money in an attempt to recoup losses.

Compulsive Gambler: a person with an impulse disorder who suffers from a chronic and progressive psychological disease; may also be called an addictive or pathological gambler; characterized by four specific features:

1. Progression: a need to bet larger amounts of money and/or take greater risks to produce the desired amount of excitement;
2. Intolerance of losing: losing is a blow to this gambler's ego, and when he loses, he continuously *chases* those losses in an attempt to eliminate negative feelings;
3. Preoccupation: thoughts of gambling become obsessive; sees gambling and winning as a way to solve all of life's problems.
4. Disregard for consequences: the *action* is all that matters; as the addiction progresses, the gambler violates all of his moral and ethical beliefs in an attempt to stay in the action and win big.

Dopamine: a chemical in the brain; a neurotransmitter that, when acting on the brain receptors, results in feelings of pleasure.

Egodystonic: the feelings experienced by the gambler as a result of his losses or other inappropriate behaviors; negative, painful, and a blow to his self-esteem.

Egosyntonic: the feelings experienced by the gambler when he wins: proud, happy, and self-assured.

Enabling: allowing the negative behavior to continue by the act of extricating the gambler from an uncomfortable, usually financial, position. There are typically three types of enablers: primary, secondary, and auxiliary.

1. Primary enabler: usually a spouse or parent; historically bails out the gambler on numerous occasions.
2. Secondary enabler: may be a family member, friend, or co-worker; unaware that he is enabling, he sees himself rather as a helper.
3. Auxiliary enabler: someone who will occasionally bail out the gambler. This may not necessarily be financial,

but rather a cover-up lie about the gambler's where
abouts, job duties, etc.

Escape Gambler: usually female; plays slot machines and other solitary
non-competitive games; often married to men who are alcoholic,
abusive, or pathological gamblers; may be depressed and gamble in this
fashion in an attempt to, at least temporarily, avoid these troublesome
areas.

External Locus of Control: the gambler's belief that his losing is the
result of some outside power; as a result, he avoids taking any responsibility for the negative outcomes of his choices.

Gamble: to risk money, or something of value, on the outcome of an
unpredictable chance event or contest.

Gambler: a person who plays at games of chance for money or something of value or takes chances on the outcome of a particular event.

Gamblers Anonymous: a self-help group for individuals with gambling
problems; founded in 1960, it views pathological gambling as a disease
and encourages each individual to admit his/her inability to control
his/her gambling and to take control of his/her life. It is modeled on the
highly successful Alcoholics Anonymous program, which preceded it.

Gam-Anon: a self-help group for the family members and friends of
the problem gambler.

Hidden disease: used to describe gambling; so called because it is not
directly detectable through observation; unlike alcohol or drug addiction, there is no stagger, smell, slurred speech, or evidence of intoxica-
tion, in fact, no obvious sign of an apparent problem.

Internal Locus of Control: the gambler's belief that his intelligence,
behavior, skill, and/or luck are directly responsible for his financial
success while gambling.

Narcissistic Personality: frequently found in problem gamblers, it reflects the following characteristics:

1. grandiosity, see themselves as special and expect to be treated as such;
2. exploit tendencies in others and use people to their advantage;
3. poor reaction to criticism and seek approval from others;
4. recurrent fantasies of success;
5. chronic feelings of envy;
6. lacking in empathy.

The narcissistic personality will present many, but not necessarily all, of the aforementioned characteristics.

Pathological Gambling: a progressive disorder characterized by a continuous or periodic loss of control over gambling; a preoccupation with gambling and with obtaining money with which to gamble; irrational thinking; and a continuation of the behavior despite adverse consequences.

Problem Gambler: a person who invests considerable time and emotional energy in gambling, or planning to do so, and who plays for stakes that are higher than he can afford. Problem gamblers may progress to compulsive gambling; however, some are able to stop or cut down on their gambling as circumstances dictate.

Professional Gambler: makes a living by gambling; skilled in the games he chooses to play, and able to control both the amount of time and money spent gambling; not addicted to gambling and reflects a positively balanced lifestyle.

Relief and Escape Gambler: gambles to find relief from feelings of anxiety, depression, anger, boredom, and loneliness; the gambling provides an analgesic effect rather than eliciting any type of euphoric response.

Recreational / Social Gambler: similar to the casual social gambler; enjoys the activity without any life interference; winning is greatly enjoyed, and losses are considered as the price one pays for the entertainment.

Serious Social Gambler: heavily involved in gambling and considers it his main source of recreation; lacks balance in his life, but gambling is still secondary to family and vocation; unlikely to develop into a compulsive gambler if he has maintained this level for a period of years.

South Oaks Gambling Screen (S.O.G.S.): a 20-question screening instrument used for diagnosis in determination of pathological gambling; introduced in 1987, it is validated and reliable; some criticisms include false positives, failure to consider frequency of gambling, does not recognize problem gamblers, and the time frame of the test is questionable.

Tolerance: an internal demand for the gambler to place increasingly larger bets, or to take greater risks, in order to produce desired levels of excitement.

Variable Ratio Schedule of Reinforcement: when rewards come occasionally and more or less at random rather than in a fixed pattern; specifically present in gambling and a major contributor to addiction.

Limitations of the Study

As referenced in this book's "Statement of Purpose," the primary focus of this book is directed toward health care professionals with intent to educate them on problem gambling and its potential for negative consequences on the individual, family, and society. And, hopefully to assist them in the decision making process of whether to appropriately treat, or refer to alternative resources, as circumstances and abilities dictate. No health care professional, lacking in proper qualifications, should take it upon themselves to use the information contained in this book for anything other than to further their knowledge as relates to the understanding of problem gambling and treatment responses to same. This should not be viewed as a "how to" book for those without training and qualifications.

The term *hidden disease* is commonly used when referring to gambling addiction. Because of the hidden nature of this problem and its having been recognized as a psychiatric disorder only since 1979, there is a dearth of research information relevant to this issue.

That being the case, the information contained in this book will reflect a non-empirical composition of some of the many theories, philosophies, and opinions of today's world of pathological gambling.

Additionally, the scope of this book limits its ability to specifically address those problems as experienced by special populations.

And, finally, even though the information contained in this book will be fairly general in nature, it should in no way be used as a self-help instrument for those individuals experiencing gambling problems.

CHAPTER TWO

Outline of the Central Chapters

<u>Introduction</u>

Tasman, Kay, and Lieberman (1997, p. 1265) says:

> DSM-IV, like DSM-III-R before it, covertly recognized the ubiquity of gambling behavior and the desire to gamble by the careful wording of criterion A for pathological gambling: "Persistent and recurrent maladaptive gambling behavior as indicated by five (or more) of the following." This definition of pathological gambling differs from some other definitions of impulse control disorders not elsewhere classified, which are worded as "failure to resist an impulse to." This difference implies that neither gambling behavior nor failure to resist an impulse to engage in it is viewed as pathological in and of itself. Rather, the maladaptive nature of the gambling behavior is the essential feature of pathological gambling and defines it as a disorder.

DSM-III-R and DSM-IV secretly recognized that gambling behavior is everywhere.

In an article by Hirshey (1994), she refers to the United States as a gambling nation and reports that, as we enter the 21st century, virtually all Americans will live within a 4-hour drive of a casino.

Again, Tasman et al. (1997) call gambling the fastest growing industry in America.

Previously cited research in Chapter 1 of this book has referenced the enigmatic status of gambling and all that surrounds it. That research has shown that gambling and its accoutrements are fraught with inconsistencies.

We are told by this research that opportunities to gamble will grow, more people will gamble, and, as a result, more problems will be experienced by those susceptible to this disorder.

What this same research does not tell us is that there will be an adequate therapeutic response available to deal with those problems. Instead, it cites a lack of treatment facilities, a shortage of qualified experienced caregivers, and no apparent sign of funding from any source directed toward these problems.

This, then, becomes the focus of the central chapters of this book:

$ To, based on current theory and research, inform and educate the reader in those areas of gambling, associative problems, and treatment considerations;

$ To examine gambling as an activity;

$ To look at who is the gambler;

$ To look at what causes and what constitutes pathological gambling;

$ To explore the impact of this disorder on the family;

$ To learn to assess and diagnose the problem; and, of course,

$ To be made fully aware of various treatment options.

Finally, there is a statement of closure discussing considerations for the future.

Gambling: The Activity

Research has shown that, in the past decade, the availability of legalized gambling, especially casino gambling, has increased dramatically in the United States. Twenty-seven states have legal casino gambling, and between 75 percent and 90 percent of Americans gamble (Pasternak, 1997).

This chapter examines that research and reports on this recent surge in the phenomenon of gambling.

It begins its examination of the modern day growth of this activity by looking at lotteries, legalization of casinos, the Indian Gaming Regulatory Act, the legalization of riverboat casinos, and a brief look at the newest component of this activity, internet gambling.

Next, it explores the reasons why people gamble. It looks at their motivation as well as what they hope to gain as a result of engaging in this behavior.

And then, it addresses the specific games in which people participate from the simplest lottery games up to those provided only by casinos. It looks at slot machines and their attraction and explores whether or not video games are possible precursors to engaging in this activity.

There is also consideration given to the efforts of Las Vegas casinos to market themselves as family vacation destinations.

And this chapter closes with a reflection of the views of local governments toward gambling in their communities.

As this activity of gambling is examined, it will be shown to be widely varied and diverse – as diverse as those who participate, and are described in the next chapter.

The Gambler

As the previous chapter indicated that current research has shown that approximately 75 percent to 90 percent of Americans gamble, this chapter looks at the specifics of those numbers.

It explores the demographic composition of America's gamblers. It looks at the elderly population and their gambling involvement. And, moving to the opposite end of the age continuum, it looks at adolescents and what role they play in the gambling culture of today.

This is followed by an examination of gender comparisons – looking at what are the percentages of male to female gamblers and what are the motivations and preferences specific to each.

Attention then turns to the six types of gamblers as referenced in Custer and Milt (1985) and the criterion specific to each, those being:

$ the professional gambler
$ the antisocial personality gambler
$ the casual social gambler
$ the serious social gambler
$ the relief and escape gambler
$ the compulsive gambler

Additional research, specifically Lesieur and Rosenthal (1991), describes gambling behavior as a four-stage progression, these being:

$ winning phase
$ losing phase
$ desperation phase
$ hopelessness

Each of these is examined addressing individual characteristics specific to each, as well as their relationship to the gambler.

This final phase of hopelessness, experienced by some gamblers, becomes the focus of the next chapter.

Pathological Gambling

Since 1980 pathological gambling has been recognized by the American Psychiatric Association as a psychiatric disorder of impulse control and was so listed in its *Diagnostic and Statistical Manual of Mental Disorder*, third edition, DSM-III.

In the last 20 years, the Diagnostic and Statistical Manual has undergone two revisions, DSM-III-R and DSM-IV, and within each, although remaining classified as an impulse disorder, the criteria defining pathological gambling has changed as well.

It is of note that some researchers have not only taken issue with this definition of pathological gambling, but have questioned the whole category of impulse disorders.

In a study by McElroy, Hudson, Pope, Keck, and Aizley (1992), they report that:

> The impulse control disorders in general remain a mysterious group of conditions. Even their diagnostic validity, individually and as a category, remains in question. Authors doubting the legitimacy of these disorders have generally argued that afflicted individuals do not really experience "irresistible" impulses, but, rather, have voluntary control over their impulsive behaviors, or that their impulsive behaviors are nonspecific symptoms secondary to other underlying psychiatric disorders (p. 323).

This position is reflective of much of the current research and theory regarding pathological gambling. The considerations of alternative diagnoses are explored within this chapter.

Regardless of the controversy regarding definition, research does indicate that pathological gambling does exist.

This chapter explores the criteria that currently defines pathological gambling as an impulse disorder as listed in DSM-IV.

In an attempt at explanation of this disorder, this chapter addresses research findings in the area of theories and causes as possible contributors to pathological gambling, as follows.

In Rosenthal (1993), his study lists what he believes are three primary components and six predisposing factors that can operate individually or in combination to cause or contribute to this disorder.

In Berman and Siegel (1992), they discuss the relationship of pathological gambling to the following theories:

$ psychological
$ learning and perception
$ cultural and sociological
$ biological
$ addiction
$ antisocial personality disorder
$ mental illness

In continuation of this area of exploration, this chapter explores Jacobs (1989) and his *General Theory of Addiction*, and Taber (1993) and his *Addictive Behavior, An Informal Clinical View*.

Pathological gambling then, as research shows, is the end result of a process – a progression through a period of time when the gambler and those around him experience the fallout from this disorder. That then becomes the area of attention of the following chapter.

The Family

This chapter addresses the relationship between the pathological gambler and his family.

Heineman (1993) describes this relationship as follows:

> The disease of compulsive gambling is an emotional illness, which leads the afflicted to believe the answer to all existing problems, financial or emotional, is to "hit it big" one more time. This childlike thinking often keeps the compulsive gambler active in his disease until the very late stages. In the meantime, the family and friends are continually affected by a behavior they cannot control and do not understand. As a result, the family may be more affected, emotionally and physically, than the compulsive gambler. Because this disease can be completely hidden for so long, the family too often has no knowledge as to the depth of the illness until the late stages (p. 596).

Further research by McGurrin (1992) indicates that, because of the progressive as well as hidden nature of this disorder, the effects on the family, especially the wife, are experienced in stages.

This chapter explores those stages and all that which occurs within each. They are, as described by McGurrin:

$ phase one, realization plus denial
$ phase two, financial crisis
$ phase three, lack of control
$ phase four, hopelessness

McGurrin goes on to address the impact of this disorder on the children in the family, and this chapter examines what those effects are, as well as the children's response to this issue in their lives.

Additional research in this area by Lorenz and Yaffee (1988) is addressed, citing the psychosomatic, emotional, and marital difficulties experienced by the spouse of the pathological gambler, as will that of Lesieur (1992) in which he reports on the signs of psychosocial maladjustment exhibited by the children of pathological gamblers.

In Miller (1996) he calls pathological gambling a hidden disease – hidden because there are no obvious signs of this disorder. A hidden disorder that, because of its nature, destroys not only the life of the person experiencing the problem, but specifically the lives of his family and all those who care about him as well.

Because of the dramatic impact of this problem, the obvious goal in this situation becomes the focus of the next chapter, "Assessing the Problem."

Assessing the Problem

The function of this chapter is to describe a process of data collection that, when collectively interpreted, locates the affected individual at a specific point of progression on the continuum of the disorder of pathological gambling.

The chapter begins with defining the clinical criteria that constitutes pathological gambling as found in the *Diagnostic and Statistical Manual of Mental Disorders*, fourth edition, DSM-IV (p. 618) under Impulse-Control Disorders Not Elsewhere Classified.

Next is an examination of what Glazer (1998) calls the only reliable, validated screening instrument currently in use to identify pathological gamblers, the South Oaks Gambling Screen.

In addition to the presenting issues of pathological gambling, research shows that individuals affected by this disorder frequently experience a high rate of comorbidity with several other psychiatric disorders and conditions.

In that regard, this chapter looks to Tasman, Kay, and Lieberman (1997) in which they cite studies identifying, not only the comorbidity issues, but the frequency of occurrence found in the pathological gambler at the time of assessment. Additionally, Levy and Feinberg (1991) report significant findings of comorbidity issues among a population of hospitalized gambling patients. Other studies – specifically, Rosenthal (1992), which addresses second addictions as simultaneous or sequential, and Jacobs (1991) which reports on his evaluation of alcohol and drug patients for concurrent gambling problems – are explored.

Another area of concern addressed in this chapter is found in Miller (1996) in which he reports on the pathological gambler presenting for treatment of another disorder, either psychological or physiological.

Here is where Pasternak (1997) suggests that an indirect method of questioning may be appropriate in the pursuit of a comprehensive assessment.

Upon completion of collection and interpretation of assessment data, attention can be turned to considerations of the next chapter, *Treatment*.

Treatment

"Research evidence suggests that the processes leading to pathological gambling involve a complex and dynamic interaction between ecological, psychophysiological, developmental, cognitive, and behavioral components" (Blasyczynski and Silove, 1995, p. 196).

This study goes on to report that the absence of a unifying theory related to pathological gambling has resulted in many varied approaches to its treatment.

In McGurrin (1992) he reports that current information on proper treatment of this disorder is tentative and incomplete, and, because of this, those treating pathological gamblers should appreciate their own clinical observations and insights.

Based on this information, this chapter explores those various treatment options as reflected in current research.

It looks at the two modalities available for treatment of this disorder – inpatient hospitalization and outpatient services – and addresses specific criteria considerations for placement as found in Rosenthal (1992).

Establishing therapeutic goals for the pathological gambler, as referenced in Tasman, Kay, and Lieberman (1997), will be explored, as will the methods available to address those goals. Specifically, in Walker (1993) he provides information on:

$ Gamblers Anonymous
$ group psychotherapy
$ conjoint marital therapy
$ psychoanalysis
$ aversion therapy
$ behavioral counseling
$ cognitively based treatment strategies

Additionally, this chapter looks at the most common form of outpatient treatment currently in use, that being Miller's (1986) Four-Phase Approach. This is a process where the pathological gambler chooses to lose his addiction to gambling, while mourning that loss. Those phases are as follows:

$ phase one, getting the gambler to commit to abstinence;
$ phase two, getting the gambler to identify and confront the problems that have been caused by gambling;
$ phase three, getting the gambler to focus on longer-term problems;
$ phase four, getting the gambler to recognize personal limitations in regard to control of gambling behaviors.

This chapter then looks at the process of treatment planning. Having the diagnostic criteria relevant to the pathological gambler and being aware of the various treatment modalities and methods available, it is now that, as McGurrin (1992) said, the professional treating this disorder must appreciate his own clinical observations and insights and personally assess the strengths, weaknesses, and needs of the pathological gambler.

In response, this chapter presents a hypothetical treatment plan designed to meet those needs, this plan being a six-part consideration of:

$ personal, therapeutic, and educational
$ interpersonal
$ financial
$ legal
$ professional/vocational
$ relapse prevention

With each of these sections being comprehensively detailed.

Finally, this chapter looks at the "success" rates of treating patholog-ical gambling as reported in Pasternak (1997) and *The Harvard Mental Health Letter* (January 1996).

Attention then moves to the last chapter of this book, *Discussion*.

Discussion

Twelve million Americans are problem or compulsive gamblers (*Family Circle,* Feb 1, 1996).

In a study by Mobilia (1993), pathological gambling is called America's latest social addiction.

In *Policy Review* (March-April, 1996) we are told that:

$ one million adolescents are addicted to gambling;

$ ten million Americans have a habit that is out of control;

$ when gambling activities are legalized and made accessi-ble, the number of addicted gamblers increases from 100 to 550 percent; and

$ gambling is this nation's fastest growing addictive behavior.

Franklin and Ciarrocchi (1987) say that "developing professional competence in treating pathological gambling is a problem because of the scarcity of treatment programs" (p. 60).

And *The Alcoholism and Drug Abuse Weekly* (June 28, 1999) reports that "the National Gambling Impact Study Commission Report released this month concluded that government and private sector efforts to treat gambling addiction have been inadequate, leaving the field without a proven treatment approach for problem gamblers." (p. 1).

Research cited throughout the previous chapters of this book has shown that opportunities to gamble are growing, and with that growth the potential for pathological gambling to occur increases as well. And, this research implies that this proliferation, in combination with inade-quate treatment resources, is destined to pose a significant social problem in America.

This final chapter looks at various research recommendations in response to dealing with this potential threat.

It looks at the National Gambling Impact Study Commission Report in which they identify current barriers to treatment services while providing recommendations for the increase of, and access to, such serv-ices.

Additionally, there is an examination of the proposed prophylactic measures by Lesieur (1992) in his response to the potential problems of pathological gambling.

And, in conclusion, this chapter addresses future research needs as referenced in Glazer (1998), Spunt, Dupont, Lesieur, Liberty, and Hunt (1998), as well as those of McGurrin (1992) in which he provides a list of 13 issues currently being debated within the field and suggests that some definitive research in each of these areas would ultimately lead to a greater understanding of this disorder of pathological gambling.

CHAPTER THREE

Gambling: The Activity

In a study by Miller (1996, p. 623-624) the activity of gambling is described as follows:

> Gambling can be viewed as placing at risk something of value with the expectation that a behavior one chooses will produce a return of something of greater value. Gambling differs from investing to the extent that chance events actually determine the outcome of a gambling process, and it is not the skill of the party placing the bet that determines the outcome of the event in question.

An additional study regarding the activity of gambling by McGurrin (1992) states that the behavior of human beings wagering on the outcome of chance events has been historically documented for at least the last 6000 years. He goes on to say that the most recent professional interest in both normal and pathological gambling in the United States is clearly a function of the astonishingly rapid expansion of legal opportunities to gamble and the diversification of the situations and games of chance upon which one may wager.

In support of this position, Volberg (1993) has addressed some of these issues specific to the expansion and growth of gambling opportunities in the United States.

Her study stated that since the 1970s, legalized gambling has gained in popularity and legitimacy in the United States. Private sector gambling industries have grown rapidly, as have state-sponsored gambling activities. Also, states experiencing financial problems have legalized lotteries, parimutuel racing, and off-track betting in an effort to generate revenue. Between 1964 and 1989, 33 states authorized lotteries.

In 1976, New Jersey became the second state to legalize casinos, and the first state to do so since Nevada legalized casinos in 1931. In 1988, the federal government passed the Indian Gaming Regulatory Act, intended to legislate relations between state governments and American Indian Tribes regarding gambling on tribal lands. In 1989 and 1990, Iowa, Illinois, and Mississippi legalized river boat casinos, followed closely by Louisiana in 1991. In 1989, shipboard casinos were operating on cruise ships sailing out of American ports in California, Florida, and the Gulf Coast States.

Volberg goes on to say that in 1989, Americans wagered $290 billion on legal and illegal games, including parimutuels, lotteries, casinos, legal bookmaking, cardrooms, charitable games, Indian high-stakes bingo, and illegal games such as the numbers and sports betting. The gross win, or total revenues from this gaming for the operators was approximately $25 billion. Two thirds (67%) of all monies wagered was gambled at slot machines and casino tables in Nevada and New Jersey. Parimutuel wagers as well as on- and off-track wagering on horses and dogs accounted for 6% of the gross annual wager. Lotteries accounted for another 7% of this sum. Americans increased the amount they wagered between 1982 and 1989 by nearly $140 billion.

Volberg cites a study by Christensen (1990), which states that since 1982, gambling has outpaced the American economy in terms of the percentage of personal income spent on wagering compared to other goods and services.

Further evidence reflecting this prevalence, growth, and expansion of gambling is found in the following studies.

Viets and Miller (1997) refer to the expansion of the gambling industry as clearly broadening the number of opportunities to gamble, addressing specifically the recent legalization of gambling sites on Native American land and on river boats, which has led to the opening of more than 170 new casinos across America in the last seven years. Concurrently, they cite a study by Lesieur and Rosenthal (1991), in which it was reported that during that year, 1991, 80% of the United States population was gambling, in contrast to 61% of this same population gambling when polled two decades earlier.

Continuing this position, Pasternak (1997) has stated that in the past decade, the availability of legalized gambling, especially casino gambling, has proliferated in the United States. Currently, some form of legalized gambling exists in every state in the Union, except Utah and Hawaii, with 27 states having legalized casino gambling. This study goes on to say that overall, between 75 and 90 percent of Americans gamble, and in 1996, they wagered a total of $586.5 billion on all forms of legal gambling in the United States.

A 1996 study by Reno supports these numbers saying that the 500 billion dollars plus that Americans legally waged in 1996 was more than was collectively spent on groceries in the United States. This dollar amount represented a 3000 percent increase in legal wagers since 1976.

Rose (1995) presents this gambling explosion in an even more global concept. He states that legal commercial gambling is one of the fastest growing industries not only in the United States but in the world. In part this is because it is starting from a base of virtually zero, so the year-to-year percentage increases are spectacular, but the numbers in absolute dollars are equally impressive.

In looking at the precipitators for this new growth of gambling in the United States, we begin with a study by Eadington (1995), in which he addresses the historical process of change of attitude toward gambling and its legal presence. He reports that what had recently been considered a sin, a vice, a deviant form of behavior, an outlaw industry, is now frequently being presented as a legitimate form of adult entertainment. A catalyst for economic development or redevelopment, a source for badly needed revenues for governments or charities, and a creator of jobs for depressed communities. The legalization of gambling became a major tool for planners and politicians to address broad social and economic problems confronting their jurisdictions and their constituencies. Problems it seemed that could not be solved by other more traditional strategies.

In keeping with this line of thought, Stoil (1994) indicates that this change in the past 50 years has not been a mere loosening of restrictions on legal gambling, but rather a massive shift in national attitudes toward the activity. Whereas forty years ago, gambling was viewed as an act of greed preying on the weaknesses of others and associated with organized crime, we now have casino gambling and lotteries promoted by local governments as an act of civic responsibility.

In Reno (1996), the role of local government in this activity of gambling is addressed. This study shows that in 1994, government received $1.4 billion from casinos alone while lotteries contributed another $10 billion to state coffers. These types of numbers prompted state legislatures to consider more than 1,600 additional gambling-related bills.

And finally, Rosenthal (1995) says that the drive for new casinos and casino gambling has roots in an economic downturn accompanied by budgetary problems for state and local government.

This recent growth phenomenon as regards to the activity of gambling presents an obvious question, why? Why is it that the American public is so tolerant of, and participates to such a degree in this new wave of gambling?

"Most people gamble for fun, relaxation, and escape from the pressures of their daily lives." (Heineman, 1992, p. XVIII).

Berman and Siegel (1992) state that their study found that games of chance in which money is at risk hold a special fascination for most people. These games offer fun, excitement, a change of pace, and of course always that opportunity to try our luck at improving our lots in life.

Miller (1996) says people gamble for social interaction and entertainment. He states that the setting of a casino creates a unique atmosphere of visual and auditory stimulation. The operational sounds combined with those of the participants can provide an almost hypnotic state allowing the individual player to become detached from their usual frame of reference and life stressors.

Ocean and Smith (1993) present in their study another view of casinos. They report that they found that the more human needs that are met by an institution, the more complete the institution. And, a gambling institution, casino, is a place where players can not only gamble, but eat, drink, meet friends and even find sexual companions.

Having examined existing research regarding reasons people gamble, attention now turns to a further exploration of research for an explanation of the venues which people choose to participate in this activity. Primary to which are casinos, the lotteries, and the newest option, the internet, electronic technology.

Previously addressed research has shown that the recent growth of casino gambling in the United States has been unprecedented. Miller (1997) reports 170 casino openings in the last seven years. This research has also shown that most of these casinos are properties of the Native Americans and have developed as a result of the Indian gaming regulation act of 1988.

Hoil (1994) claims that the Indian Gaming Regulation Act of 1988 is considered by some to be the greatest impetus to the national pro-gambling climate. The act requires tribes to negotiate agreements or compacts with state governments affecting the distribution of revenue from gambling, but makes it difficult for states to refuse to permit casinos on reservation land. Amendments to this act essentially force states to accept such compacts or have their authority to negotiate legally co-opted by the federal government.

In Rose (1992), this position is supported where he says that this act accounts for a business that has gone from zero to billions of dollars per year in wagers in just over a decade, and is considered to be the fastest growing industry in the world.

However, there has been a downside to this rampant growth of casino gambling. In returning to Stoil (1994), he states that unfortunately this government-sponsored rush for greater access to legal gambling is not matched by government interest in prevention of its adverse public health consequences as there is no consideration for provisions to attempt to prevent or treat compulsive gambling included in this legislation.

Research points out similar experiences with those communities embracing the river boat casinos. Goldstein (1997) describes the advent of the river boat casinos in Missouri, saying that people were told that there would be nostalgic old time river boats that would conduct gambling during river cruises. Instead, they have massive casinos decorated to look like boats, with no engines in them, located off the river in man-made pools.

Moving to consideration of lotteries, Mikesell (1990) reports that lotteries give states direct revenue from the commercial gambling market. That 32 states plus the District of Columbia, encompassing almost three quarters of the U.S. population, operate games. A dramatic increase since the first modern day lottery of 1964 New Hampshire.

Mikesell goes on to say that lotteries are pure games of chance. Winners are picked solely at random, so player skill is not a factor. Some major lottery games have parimutuel prizes, or prizes determined by the amount of dollars wagered on that game. In that case, the larger the amount wagered, the greater the prize, and larger prizes promote greater amounts of wagering.

In a supportive article by Kaplan (1990), the lotteries are described as an activity the public enjoys and state legislatures have become wedded to them. The cheap high they offer feeds the dream for materialism, and despite their inability to solve all the financial problems of states, the money they contribute to state coffers allows politicians to avoid the proposal of additional taxes. Kaplan is very emphatic about saying "One thing is certain about lotteries, they are here to stay."

An article by Braidfoot (1988) reflects the attitudes and opinions of those opposed to the lotteries. They argue against them because they find them to be regressive, to contribute to increased incidences of illegal gambling as well as compulsive gambling, to involve exploitation of ethnic and minority groups, and to involve the state in a paradoxical role of profiting from its citizens in a business activity which it conducts with extensive marketing and advertising.

An example of this is found in a study by Reno (1996), in which it is reported that in that year the legal wager in the U.S. was in excess of $500 billion, and that state and local governments, in an attempt to gain a share of this wager, advertised their lottery games with a total expenditure of $350 million.

In the examination of the last of the venues, the new computer technology is described by Shaffer (1996) as the modern means by which gambling is delivered to homes, businesses, and airplanes. This study states that researchers estimate there are 13 to 15 million internet users in the United States and through the use of credit cards and new computer technology access becomes easy while opportunity is everywhere.

A study by Griffiths (1996) states that these new technologies may provide many people with their first exposure to the world of gambling and could realistically be much more enticing than previous non-technological opportunities.

Griffith goes on to warn of dangers inherent in this medium, those being technological addictions. These addictions are operationally defined as non-chemical, or behavioral addictions that involve human and machine interaction. They can either be passive, such as television, or active, such as computer games, and usually contain inducing and reinforcing features that may contribute to the promotion of addictive tendencies. Although at this time, there is little empirical evidence of technological addictions as distinct clinical entities. Griffiths states that extrapolations from research indicate that they do and will exist. Further exploration of Shaffer (1996) states that inherent in the process of this new computer technology is the fact that internet gambling is difficult to regulate in that there is no specific jurisdiction responsible for its activities, and a legitimate concern that this new technology may increase gambling addiction.

In a related article by Gupta and Derevensky (1996), the relationship between video games and internet gambling is addressed. This study reported that commercial video games and internet gambling activities have similar attractive features and reinforcement schedules. And, the study suggests that video game playing may be a precursor to the playing of slot machines. It states that both the video games and games of chance are exciting, they both contain elements of randomness, and both operate on schedules of intermittent reinforcement. The one major difference identified by this study is that video games provide feedback allowing a player to improve performance and exhibit some degree of control, while most gambling situations do not involve skill.

The games of chance and their attraction are further described in the following studies. In Miller (1996), this study was directed to casinos and their card and table games, along with their primary attraction, the slot machine. Miller states that the casino table games, in addition to the gambling attraction, offer a very positive social experience, whereas slot machine play is quite isolative. Their attraction is that they are operationally fast, aurally and visually stimulating, require a low initial investment, provide frequent wins, require no specific knowledge to play, and may be played alone.

In Griffiths (1996), it is a similar story. This study reports on a version of similar activities as those related to the playing of slot machines. It addresses the structured characteristics of internet gambling which promote interactivity and define alternative realities to the user allowing them feeling of anonymity that may be very psychologically rewarding to certain individuals.

And Eadington (1987) addresses the allure of the lottery as, even though it is a game of chance with an extremely high negative probability, it remains a simple, low-risk, high-reward opportunity.

Previously cited research has shown that there are billions of dollars wagered on gambling activity annually in the United States. And, in Reno (1996), it was pointed out that state and local governments spend a great deal of money, $350 million in 1996, in advertising dollars in pursuit of a share of those billions.

They are not alone. Las Vegas, Nevada, with its legalized casino market is making a concerted effort in an attempt to attract new gambling customers as well. In Jones (1996), the efforts of casino marketing are addressed. A virtual explosion of new casinos is opening, with each being more opulent than the one before. Each is vying for their share of the gambling dollar, with many marketing themselves as family vacation spots by adding theme parks and other similar attractions.

A supporting study by Ogintz (2000) reports that three million children currently accompany families to Las Vegas each year. Many casinos provide day care centers for these children complete with climbing structures, computers, video games, Barbie doll houses, and movies on giant screen televisions. The centers are staffed by trained counselors and employ a realistic staff-to-child ratio, and charges are minimal to those guests participating in the activities of the casino.

The activity of gambling.

CHAPTER FOUR

The Gambler

Morgan (1993) advised psychologists and other professionals to recognize gambling behavior as a continuum from total abstinence to occasional gambling, to moderate gambling, and finally to heavy gambling which ultimately leads to problems.

Many different behaviors within a singularly defined behavior. This is also true when applied to the gambler. No one definition describes those individuals who participate in the activity of gambling. Instead, they are diverse. In a study by Custer and Milt (1985), they identify and define six different types of gambler.

1. The professional gambler makes his living by gambling and so considers it his profession. He is very proficient in the games he plays and is able to control both the amount of money and the time spent gambling. Significant others may express concern about his lifestyle, but the professional gambler is not addicted to gambling. He usually leads a very balanced lifestyle and keeps family and finances in proper perspective. His self-esteem is derived from a multiplicity of sources and is not dependent on the outcome of his gambling.

2. The antisocial or criminal gambler, in contrast to the professional gambler, uses gambling as a way to cheat or swindle others. He is likely to be currently involved in several ongoing illegal activities, and have a long history of antisocial behavior. He may also have a history of unstable relationships, as well as poor academic and/or work performance. When in trouble, he may try to get involved in the mental health system in an attempt

to be diagnosed as a compulsive gambler, and try to use this as a legal defense.

3. The casual social gambler gambles for recreation and excitement. Although he attempts to win, and obviously enjoys it when it happens, he considers his losses as the cost of his entertainment. There is little or no ego involvement in winning or losing, and his gambling does not interfere with family or vocational obligations.

4. The serious social gambler is more likely to invest more of his ego in gambling than the casual social gambler. He has less balance in his life, may have difficulty meeting personal responsibilities, and considers gambling to be his main form of recreation. Even though he is heavily involved and preoccupied with gambling, this individual still considers gambling less significant than family and vocation. This type of gambler could be compared to an individual who is intensely involved in a hobby or a sport. Problems may arise in the family over amounts of time and money spent by the gambler in pursuit of his activity even though he has not experienced a loss of control. This serious social gambler is very unlikely to develop into a compulsive gambler if he has been able to maintain his current level of involvement over a period of time, usually years.

5. The relief and escape gambler has more pathological features than the social gambler because he gambles to find relief from feelings of anxiety, depression, anger, boredom, and loneliness. There is a binge aspect to his gambling that reflects a habitual way of dealing with negative emotional states. His gambling provides him with an analgesic effect rather than any type of euphoric response. This type of gambler is in need of treatment, but not for his gambling. The gambling behavior is stable and not indicative of problem progression.

6. Compulsive gambler. There are four essential features exhibited in the behavior of the compulsive gambler. They are as follows:
    a. Progressive: The compulsive gambler is usually unable to quit even when he is ahead of the game and will continue to gamble as long as he has money. He develops an unrealistic grandiosity regarding winning, and the time spent gambling increases as does the amount of

monies spent. He has a need to bet larger amounts, as well as take greater risks, in order to produce the desired levels of excitement.

b.   Intolerance of losing: When losses occur, the compulsive gambler chases the lost money. He cannot accept normal losses because this is a blow to his grandiosity and subsequently results in a loss of self-esteem. When he loses, he abandons his gambling plan, or strategy, and pursues one goal, the big win. He hides his losses from his family and lying becomes a major tool in his gambling cycle.

c.   Preoccupation: His thoughts about gambling become a constant obsession. He looks at gambling as a way to solve not only financial, but other problems in his life as well. The pursuit of this goal, the big win, brings on a single-minded focus that not only drives him toward the success he seeks, but also serves as a defense mechanism against the troubled reality of his own life.

d.   Disregard for consequences: This is the final stage. This gambler will break his own moral and ethical prohibitions in an attempt to continue his gambling activities, avoid the destruction of his self-esteem, as well as protect his existing financial resources. It is during this period of time that forgery, theft, and embezzlement become commonplace. Even during the commission of these illegal acts, the gambler's intent is to win big and then rectify all the problems.

The study goes on to say that this gambler type is affected by four emotional needs that significantly contribute to his motivation to gamble. He is in need of affection, approval, recognition, and self-confidence. If these needs are not met by success in his gambling activity, he feels inadequate, rejected, helpless, and overwhelmed. Presented with this emotional pain, his response is to gamble in an attempt toward its elimination. This effort then usually leads to further losses, more pain, etc., the potential for an extremely negative downward spiral of compulsive behavior that may eventually lead to addiction.

One of the defining characteristics of compulsive or pathological gambling is its progression. In Lesieur and Rosenthal (1991), they have examined this progression and broken it down into four phases that they labeled winning, losing, desperation, and hopelessness. They are described as follows:

$ Winning: Male compulsive gamblers are more likely to experi-
ence a winning phase than their female counterparts. This stems
from the fact that many men get involved in gambling because
they are good at it and receive peer recognition for their early
successes. The traits that foster this are their competitiveness,
high energy, ability with numbers, and interest in the strategies of
the various games. Some may win simply because they were
lucky. Much of their self-esteem derives from gambling, and they
tend to spend more and more time at it in pursuit of not only
their fantasy of the big win, but also to meet their personal needs
for success and recognition.

$ Losing: In this phase the gambler may experience a run of bad
luck, or simply discover that to them losing is intolerable. This is
when the behavior known as chasing begins. All rational strategies are abandoned and the gambler tries to win everything back
at once. They panic, and bets are larger and more frequent in an
attempt to recoup their losses. This chasing is directed at not just
regaining lost monies, but at denying their helplessness, eliminat-
ing their shame and humiliation, and erasing the losing experience which provoked such feelings. Outside the gambling behavior, only their most essential debts are paid in order to have
monies to continue to gamble. Covering up and lying about their
gambling becomes more frequent. Family relationships deteriorate. Vocations are exploited for gambling opportunities (i.e.,
time, money). The gambler uses all available cash resources and
may begin to borrow. Eventually this comes to an end. They can
borrow no more and may be faced with loss of job and/or
marriage. The gambler usually confesses during this time and
pleads for forgiveness and a bailout. Somehow debts get paid and
the family, in return, gets a promise that the gambling will stop.
This may happen for a while, but usually the gambler feels that
they've gotten away with something, returns to gambling, bets
more than before, and ultimately loses all control.

$ Desperation: Now is when the gambler may start to do things
such as writing bad checks, stealing from an employer, and other
illegal activities. Once they have begun this type of behavior, it is
very easy for them to continue as they justify their actions to
themselves by saying that as soon as they hit the big win they will
make everything right. Their time is spent in their pursuit of
these illegal activities and gambling. When reminded of respon-

sibilities, or put in touch with guilt feelings, they are quick-
tempered and often abusive to those who stimulate these feel
ings. They begin to deteriorate physically as well as psychologically and morally. They frequently entertain the fantasy of starting a new life with a new name and a new identity.

$ Hopelessness: Here the gambler begins to realize that, no matter
    what, they will never get back to even again, but they no longer
    care. Now they just want to play. Their play turns sloppy and
    they lose, just as they knew they would. They just want the
    action and excitement of playing and will gamble to the point of
    complete exhaustion. It is in this phase that most who seek help
    receive it. It may come from the intervention of concerned
    family members or friends, or the behavior of the gambler
    himself as many in this phase suffer from stress-related illnesses,
    depression and suicidal ideation and attempts.

In the past quarter century the numbers of people gambling in the
United States has grown significantly. A study by Lesieur (1992) indicated that in 1974, 61% of the adult population of the U.S. gambled. In
1989, this number had increased to 71%. A follow-up study by Pasternak
(1997) saw his reported numbers to be between 75% and 90% of adult
Americans participating in some form of gambling behavior.

Of this number, two-thirds of the gambling population was male,
while one-third was female.

These numbers prompted researchers to look at the roles of men, and
especially women, as related to their gambling behavior.

Hraba and Lee (1996) found that any evidence on gender comparison
was indeed rare. They did find prevalence studies showing that more
than one half of adult American women gamble and that approximately
one third of the nation's problem gamblers were women. They found
that the woman's scope of gambling is less than that of men. They prefer
legal to illegal betting and gravitate toward non-action games such as
bingo and slot machines. And, on average they usually wager less than
men.

In a supporting study by Rosenthal (1992), he reports that women
start gambling later in life often after adult roles have been established.
They are more apt to be depressed, and gamble more for escape than
action or excitement. They play less-competitive games in which luck
plays a greater role than skill, and they play alone.

Although typically starting to gamble later in life, the onset of problems occurs very rapidly in some women. McCollum (1996) reports that

studies have shown that the difference between a male gambler and a female gambler is that it takes 15 to 20 years for a man to become a pathological gambler, but for a woman it takes only three to four years. Reasons for this being that men have been exposed to gambling activities their whole lives, from card games to odds on sporting events, whereas women have not grown up with these same experiences and the feelings of gambling, and especially winning, are new and very appealing.

Current estimates, Reno (1996) reports, are that an estimated 10 to 12 million Americans have a gambling habit that is out of control. On the opposite ends of the age continuum of gambling behaviors in the U.S. are the elderly and the adolescent. In Jacobi (1996), it is reported that compulsive gambling behavior is increasing among both teenagers and the elderly, and for similar reasons. Gambling provides feelings of excitement and distraction from depression and loneliness.

A study by Fessler (1996) states that, to date, no national study has been done to document the rising problem of gambling and the elderly, but various regional studies have reported an incidence of elderly gambling problems ranging from 5% to 10% with Florida being the highest at 16.8%.

Due to the age of the adolescent gambler it is difficult to acquire specific numbers as their gambling is not of a legally recognized age appropriate behavior, however, problem estimates do exist.

Jacobs (1989) estimates in the past year more than half of all teenagers have wagered on some event or game of chance, and there are currently as many as one million juveniles in this country with serious gambling problems. The study goes on to say that 4% to 6% of these adolescents meet diagnostic criteria for a diagnosis of pathological gambling. This is as much as three times the current rate of adults with this same disorder.

These numbers are supported by McGurrin (1992), in which he reports that in 1988 as many as seven million adolescents were frequent gamblers and about one million were experiencing problems.

Previously cited research reflects the general attitude of acceptance and indeed governmental encouragement for the activity of gambling. However, this behavior is not without a price. Burke (1996) reports that the costs to society keep increasing. The revenues raised by legal gambling are largely, if not entirely, offset by the costs created by problem gambling, such as insurance fraud, embezzlement, and imprisonment. This study goes on to estimate that each pathological gambler costs society anywhere from $13,000 to $52,000.

Abt and McGurrin (1992) report that gambling is both accepted and condemned in the United States, and thus reflects the conflicts in American values. They go on to say that:

Sometimes the gambler wins, sometimes the gambler loses, but it is the play of the game according to cultural rules that gives the gambling its meaning. Culture is an assemblage of texts explicating, among other things, that it is worth taking risks. The gambling ritual symbolically affirms that society and life are built on cycles of despair and triumph, and the text for this revelation is encapsulated in games. (p. 417).

CHAPTER FIVE

Pathological Gambling

The *Diagnostic and Statistical Manual of Mental Disorders* DSM-IV 4th edition (1994) lists pathological gambling in the category of impulse-control disorders not elsewhere classified, and describes its diagnostic features as follows:

The essential feature of pathological gambling is persistent and recurrent maladaptive gambling behavior (Criterion A) that disrupts personal, family, or vocational pursuits. The diagnosis is not made if the gambling behavior is better accounted for by a Manic Episode (Criterion B) (p. 615).

In Tasman, Kay and Lieberman (1997), they report that pathological gambling has been included in DSM-III, DSM-III-R, and DSM-IV as a disorder of impulse control. However, pathological gambling can also be viewed as an addictive disorder, an affective spectrum disorder, and an obsessive-compulsive spectrum disorder. The current DSM-IV maintains a close relationship between pathological gambling and addictive disorders, and some of its diagnostic criteria for pathological gambling were intentionally made to resemble criteria for substance abuse.

A study by Miller (1996) states that pathological gambling was first described as a formal disorder when the American Psychiatric Association included it in the third edition of its *Diagnostic and Statistical Manual* (DSM-III, 1980). It was considered to be a disorder of impulse control.

This study goes on to say that although lay terminology frequently refers to this condition as compulsive gambling, it is really not a variant of an obsessive compulsive disorder, the individual is engaged in a behavior that involves anxiety and they would prefer not to be involved in the behavior. As for pathological gamblers, they enjoy gambling except at the very end stages of their problem.

Miller continues his study stating that when the American Psychiatric Association revised its Diagnostic and Statistical Manual in 1987 (DSM-III-R, 1987), it specifically modeled the diagnostic criteria for pathological gambling after those for psychoactive substance abuse. Those being a preoccupation with gambling, increasing use, quantities and frequencies of use that exceeded intent, unsuccessful efforts to cut back or stop the behavior and persistence of use despite adverse consequences.

And, the most recent edition of this diagnostic manual (DSM-IV, 1994) continues to use the term "pathological gambling" rather than "gambling addiction," and still classifies the disorder as a disorder of impulse control, but it focuses on features that are similar to features of substance abuse and dependence.

In a related study by McElroy, Hudson, Pope, Harrison, Neck, and Aizley (1992), they describe impulse control disorders as mental disorders characterized by irresistible impulses to perform harmful acts. They are defined by three essential features: (1) failure to resist an impulse, drive, or temptation to perform some act that is harmful to the person or others; (2) an increasing sense of tension or arousal before committing the act and; (3) an experience of pleasure, gratification, or release at the time the act is committed. Additionally, there may or may not be a conscious resistance to the impulse, the act may or may not be premeditated, and immediately after the act, there may or may not be regret or guilt, thereby making the behavior either egosyntonic and/or egodystonic.

The study goes on to say that the impulse control disorders as a group remain poorly studied. Except for alcohol and psychoactive substance abuse, little is known about them in terms of prevalence, demographic characteristics, course, associated psychopathology, family history, or response to treatment.

Rosenthal (1992) states simply that pathological gambling's definition is similar to that of alcohol and substance abuse. It is defined as a progressive disorder characterized by a continuous or periodic loss of control over gambling, a preoccupation with gambling and with obtaining money with which to gamble, irrational thinking, and a continuation of the behavior despite adverse consequences. This definition with its loss of control, progression, preoccupation, and disregard for consequences is similar to that for alcohol and substance dependence.

In Ciarrocchi, Kirschner, and Fallik (1991), they report that they are intrigued by the degree to which pathological gambling resembles alcoholism or other addictions. They found it interesting in that theoretically the concept is that pathological gambling is an example of a so-called pure addiction, involving no ingestion of any substance to establish an addictive cycle. And, as such, pathological gambling presents a unique opportunity to study addictive behavior without having to separate it from the effects of chemical agents.

In the Harvard Mental Health Letter (Jan 1996), they say that in DSM-IV pathological gambling is grouped, with pyromania and klepto-mania, as an impulse of disorder not elsewhere classified. However, the behavior of compulsive gamblers most resembles that of alcohol and drug dependence.

And Blume (1995) reports that even though pathological gambling has been conceptualized in several theoretical frameworks, it is widely understood as an addiction to the altered psychological state experienced while the gambler is in action.

In looking to these theories of which Blume refers to, we begin with Rosenthal (1993). In this study he refers to compulsive or pathological gambling as basically an addiction to a false state of mind.

In his contributions to the cause of this pathological gambling, he lists the following three vital components:

1. An intolerable-feeling state of helplessness, depression, or guilt. The affected individual may feel he is being pulled in two direc-tions at the same time, leading to a sense of futility about doing anything. He feels that whatever he does, it's not enough. He, himself, is never good enough. Or, he feels unlovable. Some have an enormous sense of guilt, and all seem to suffer greatly from a lack of self-esteem.
2. A highly developed capacity for self-deception. There is an omnipotence working in conjunction with other types of magical and superstitious thinking. There is a very early pattern of lying to self and a belief that through gambling his problems can be avoided.
3. Exposure to gambling under circumstances in which it is valued. The compulsive gambler most likely learned this behavior in his own family. It may have been taught by a parent, which may have provided the only togetherness they experienced. So, when the individual's gambling efforts were successful it brought recognition and status.

This study goes on to list the following as possible predisposing factors to the condition of pathological gambling:

1. A family history of compulsive gambling, with as many as one-third of identified compulsive gamblers having a biological rela-tive with the disorder.

2. Growing up in a family with an extremely critical, rejecting, or emotionally unavailable parent. For men, this is usually the father, and as such there is a concerted effort to please that parent and win their approval.
3. An emphasis in the family on status, or an overvaluing of money. Many pathological gamblers were taught at an early age to equate self-worth with money, power, or control.
4. Men, in particular, having been brought up to be extremely competitive, usually by their fathers stressing that winning is everything.
5. The existence of an early physical or developmental problem. Relevant to those who are compensating for some physical or developmental problem that caused them great shame or humiliation early in life.
6. Hyperactivity. For many experiencing Attention Deficit Hyperactive Disorder, gambling initially may provide a specific self-medication.

In continuation of the exploration of the various theories that are considered to be at least in part contributing causes to addictive behavior, the following have been presented by Berman and Siegel (1992).

Psychological Theories. The early formative years of those individuals who later show tendencies toward gambling addiction are significant in this theory. Either too much or too little parenting and early nurturing that didn't meet the early basic needs of the potential gambler may lead to prolonged frustration, a reliance on omnipotence, and potential for escape into magical thinking. Some children grow up in an unpredictable, unstable, or over-controlled home. They have little or no control personally, and as a result may become anxious and ineffectual, and consequently struggle through life trying to become masterful.

An additional consideration in this theory is that a disproportionate number of compulsive gamblers have a parent suffering from either emotional problems or their own addiction to alcohol, drugs, or gambling. And, as a result, were unable to provide the appropriate and adequate care required in the gambler's early years. Still others may have experienced the loss of a parent or care giver through death, divorce, or abandonment.

Some parents may have been critical and demanding, while others were passive and ineffective. Either way, their behavior was perceived by the gambler as rejection during the early years.

Also within this theory is the consideration of those gamblers who have a physical or developmental problem that has left them embarrassed and self-conscious resulting in a severely diminished sense of self. Feeling lonely, rejected, guilty, depressed, anxious, with little or no self-esteem, the gambler may see his gambling as an opportunity to prove to himself, and others, that he really is somebody.

And finally, this theory looks at those gamblers who are masochistic in their approach to gambling. They have a desire to lose in response to their guilt as relates to an early life loss of someone or something of importance. As a result the gambling losses put them in a place where they are comfortable with their pain.

Learning and Perception Theories. Gambling is a learned behavior, and its random reinforcement of winning sometimes and losing at others appears to insure ones continued interest in the activity. A gambler may on occasion, as a result of his winning experiences, come to believe that his individual skill is a primary factor in the outcome of these games.

Perception plays a significant role in the life of the gambler. We live in a society that places a great deal of emphasis on winning. And, of course, this holds true in gambling. Lottery winners are on television and featured in the newspapers, and gambling games boast of winners and amounts paid out, not of individuals' losses and operators' profits.

The gambler is influenced by this and thinks he is next to win. This will happen because he is special as well as skillful. If he does not win, he admits to only almost winning, never losing.

Unfortunately, one of our society's highly espoused values is extremely contraindicated when applied to gambling, yet gamblers use it and only multiply their problems. It is that old adage, "if at first you don't succeed, try, try again." Potentially very sage advice when applied appropriately, but perhaps not to gambling.

Cultural and Sociological Theories. These theories are considerations of why someone may begin to gamble, but are not defining of compulsive gambling.

Simply stated, gambling can be an accepted, or indeed valued, behavior in certain cultures and social settings. It can present entry into certain social groups where it becomes a mode of acceptance and provides a circle of ready-made friends.

Biological Theories. Supporters of this theory believe that gamblers may have a low level of serotonin (a central nervous system substance), as well as an increased responsiveness of the noradrenergic system, which is associated with poor impulse control.

Additionally, some believe that gamblers have low levels of a byproduct of the brain chemical norepinephrine, which is responsible for the regulation of arousal, thrill, and excitement. If true, this would explain the behaviors of the gamblers who complain of boredom and seek that extraordinary amount of excitement just to feel normal. And, those persons experiencing other psychological problems such as an undiagnosed depression, may medicate themselves by gambling.

Addiction Theory. This theory proposes that all addictions are similar and any substance or activity can be substituted one for another. In the case of gambling, it tends to take a predictable and progressive course if left untreated. The primary message here is that individuals addicted to gambling are at risk for other addictions as well, and may find themselves victims of multiple addictions or highly susceptible to that possibility.

Antisocial Personality Disorder Theory. These individuals reflect an early history of cruelty, lying, and stealing. Their adult patterns of behavior are inconsistent work habits, physical abuse, ignoring societal law, and an apparent lack of remorse for any offensive or inappropriate behavior. Gambling has long been considered an additional symptom of this disorder.

Mental Illness Theory. This consideration is very simple. It is thought that gambling addiction may coexist with a mental illness because it may offer the affected individual a process for socialization, or a way of dealing with the pain of his problems.

The next exploration of theory is that of Jacobs (1989) and his *General Theory of Addiction.*

This theory emphasizes the presence of two individual yet interacting predisposing factors that are held to determine whether an individual is at risk of maintaining an addictive pattern of behavior. The first of these sets is a unipolar physiological resting state that is chronically and excessively either suppressed or excited. The lifelong persistent state of hypo- or hyper-arousal is believed to predispose the individual's response to a window of stress reducing, but potentially addictive substances and/or activities.

This situation refers to that minority group of persons at either extreme of the normally distributed range of resting arousal levels. Those individuals are referred to as reduced or augmenter/enhancer types. Either of these conditions are uncomfortable and persons at these poles seek out and engage in behaviors that make them feel better.

It is to be noted that not all reducers and enhancers are prone to acquiring an addiction. This aversive physiological arousal state is only one of the two necessary predisposing conditions for developing an addiction, according to this theory.

The second precondition is a childhood and adolescence marked by deep feelings of inadequacy, inferiority, shame, guilt, and low self-esteem, combined with a feeling of rejection by parents and/or significant other. Given these conditions, one would expect behavior from that individual that was directed toward relief from this psychological distress.

So, this theory implies that those individuals with a chronically abnormal arousal rate who also tend to respond to feeling of inferiority and rejection by flight into denial and compensatory behaviors are at the highest risk for becoming addicted to whatever substance or activity they choose as their relief.

These two conditions must exist in a conducive environment and the substance or behavior chosen must do three things. It must blur reality testing by temporarily diverting ones' attention from the chronic aversive arousal state. It must lower self-criticism and self-consciousness. This occurs through an internal cognitive shift that deflects preoccupation from ones' self-perceived inadequacies. And it permits complimentary daydreams about oneself. While indulging in the potentially addictive behavior, the individual's perception of self-image is greatly enforced as is his view of social interaction and individual performance.

As the frequency and intensity of these three attributes increase, so does the possibility that the individual will cross over into a disassociative-like state.

The final theory to be examined is that of Taber (1993) and his study on *Addictive Behavior: An Informal Clinical View.*

Taber reports that his many years of working with addictive disorder patients have resulted in the following list of conclusions that he believes are relevant to those individuals suffering from chronic addictions.

$ They are, in many ways, very childish.
$ They are exceedingly unhappy most of the time.
$ If they stop one addictive behavior they will almost always either intensify other addictive behaviors or develop new ones.

$ In nearly every case they show an almost phobic aversion to normal adult values, attitudes, and habits.

$ And, as a result of these traits, they are not normal people.

Taber sees the addiction-prone individual as childish in many fundamental areas such as perception, cognition, affect, problem solving, human relations, impulse control, and self-image. He does not believe that the childishness is caused by the addictive behavior, but rather it is the childishness that makes the addiction possible.

In the areas of perception, he believes the addict to be most selective. They see what they want to see and hear what they want to hear, and are capable of distorting reality to best suit themselves.

The study goes on to say that the addict usually displays strong expectations of specialness, along with personal entitlement and magical thinking. There is an in-order-to mentality where behaviors are directed to getting somewhere else with no appreciation for here and now. The addict also experiences a great deal of negative affect, including anger, fear, and jealousy. Positive feelings are derived from participating in the addictive behavior of choice.

With this there is a cycle of mood swings, a preoccupation with getting high, or involvement in the addictive behavior, the euphoria of that temporary high, and subsequently the depression of withdrawal. They make an effort to eliminate the depression by returning to the behavior of choice and once again repeating the cycle.

The addict's problem-solving skills are limited to few, if any. Primarily choices between violent aggression and total flight or withdrawal. If there is no action taken in response to an apparent problem, he experiences frustration, anger, and self-deprecation. If, on the other hand, he responds from the opposite end of the continuum with aggression, he feels the same negative feelings compounded by guilt. Mature adult options such as discussion, examination of alternatives, compromise, and accommodation are not viable options for the addict. He wants to be controlled or in control. He fails to see himself with any degree of accuracy and often feels out of control, helpless, and overwhelmed. All of which are contributors to the continuation of the chosen addictive behavior.

In an attempt to explain the addictive person, Taber says:

Simplistic, single cause theories of addiction are plentiful and tempting. While there is, without doubt, some influence by genetic and biochemical variables in the formation of addictive behavior, it seems unlikely that there will be found to be a specific factor for each of the growing list of addictions. So intense is the devotion of some theorists to biochemical mechanisms that they reject the possibility that non-substance addictions can be considered to be addictions at all. Gambling, work, sex, spending, and other antidysphoric activities cannot be addictions, they argue, because there is no chemical to which to become addicted. This position, I believe, reflects an empty, academic and clinically naive view.

Whatever the addiction, the mood cycle is the same, the progression of use is the same, the immature personality organization is the same, the withdrawal is similar, the social consequences are equally drastic, and the tendency to be multiply addicted is the same (p. 277).

In closing this area of consideration to theory, and in support of Taber, the following is taken from Shaffer (1986).

When competing models for understanding compulsive gambling co-exist, each offering a viable explanatory system, a field experiences a crisis of concepts. Systematic research capable of resolving the crisis is delayed because the basic concepts that direct investigative research remain in chaos. To minimize this confusion, it is helpful to examine the extant models of drug and alcohol addiction, the two most studied excessive behaviors.

It is likely, at least in the short term, that the conceptual future of the compulsive gambling field will be shaped in part by the important concepts drawn from the better-known addictions. After all, we now view compulsive gambling, for better or for worse, as an addictive behavior. It is very important then that we understand and hopefully learn from the conceptual problems of the other addictions (p. 7, 8).

CHAPTER SIX

The Family

The exploration of the relationship between the pathological gambler and his family begins with a review of a study by Reno (1996).

This study reports that the scope of the problem of the impact of pathological gambling on the family is tragically underestimated due to the lack of research in this area. The limited data available comes primarily from surveys of small groups of compulsive gamblers seeking treatment, some of which follows.

A 1995 survey by the Illinois Council on Compulsive Gambling polled 200 members of Gamblers Anonymous and found that 16 percent were divorced due to their gambling addictions and another 10 percent had separated from their spouses as a result of this behavior. Reno goes on to cite an early unspecified study of spouses of compulsive gamblers, by Lorenz, in which 78 percent had threatened separation or divorce, of which 50 percent of these actually carried through with the threat. Also cited was a study by Jacobs (1989), in which 850 high school students in Southern California were surveyed and found that children of compulsive gamblers were twice as likely to experience the trauma of a broken home as compared to the norm.

This study goes on to report divorce findings from research done in Harrison County Mississippi, the hub of the state's casino industry. Here they found the number of divorces rose from 440 in 1992 to nearly 1,100 in 1993, the first full year after local legalization of casino gambling. A local Mississippi chancery court judge, William L. Stewart, claims that gambling is now a factor in about one-third of the divorce cases he currently oversees.

In addition to the dramatic impact compulsive gambling has had on separation and divorce rates, there are other significant family problems resulting from this addiction as well, those referenced as being spousal and child abuse and neglect. The Gulf Coast Women's Center in Biloxi, Mississippi, has averaged 400 additional crisis calls per month since the startup of the local casinos. Central City, Colorado, reported a sixfold rise in child protection cases in the year after casinos arrived in their community. The state's attorney for Deadwood, South Dakota, reported that children were being left in cars all night outside of casinos in their locale, while parents gambled. And Nevada led the nation in deaths of children attributable to abuse from the period 1979 to 1988, when casino gambling was illegal everywhere else except Atlantic City, New Jersey.

As well, this study notes that the children of compulsive gamblers suffer in yet another way. They have a greater propensity for substance abuse, lower academic achievement, juvenile delinquency, and mental health problems. Also, many of them are subject to developing their own gambling problems.

Another study along these lines by McGurrin (1992) reports on the dynamics of the behavior of the compulsive gambler in the conjugal family, beginning with the effects of the behavior on the spouse as described in the following phases.

The first phase is characterized by one spouse's early realization of the others gambling problems. Usually the male is the gambler, and the wife, even after recognition of the problem, attempts to deny its significance. She is easily reassured by the gambler that his behavior is not a problem, and, consequently, the husband is quite successful in concealing the extent of his gambling.

Phase two reflects the problems surrounding the financial crisis that will inevitably occur. When confronted, the husband accuses the wife of being disloyal. It is during this stage that the wife may seek money from family or friends to ease her situation. This behavior by the wife only results in allowing the gambler to continue on in his addiction. It is during this time when the wife experiences feelings of rejection and isolation, not only from her husband, but other family members and friends as she ignores their advice and refuses to leave the relationship. This is usually the precipitator to early stage depression for the wife. As this second stage continues, if there are children in the family, the wife/mother must provide explanations for the husband/father's frequent absences and seemingly uncaring behavior. The children begin to experience emotional as well as material deprivation and the mother is emotionally and physically exhausted from her unsuccessful attempts to control the gambler. She may now experience episodes of acute anxiety, confusion, resentment, as well as extended periods of depression.

Of note here is that at some time during these reactive phases of the spouse to the behavior of the compulsive gambler, she may fall victim to the phenomenon known as codependency and enabling as described in Berman and Siegal (1992).

Here they report that codependents through their behavior often encourage the behavior in the gambler that they wish to control or extinguish. This is called enabling and the following are some ways in which a spouse might enable a gambler's behavior.

$ Protection. If the gambling behavior is covered up, no one, including the gambler, has to face it.

$ Control. Attempts at control result in frustration and diminishes the self-esteem of the gambler which leads to further gambling.

$ Assuming responsibilities. In doing this, the spouse frees up the gambler to devote more time to his addiction.

$ Rationalization. If you accept the fabrications of the gambler you support his self-deception.

$ Cooperation. If you join him in gambling you lend apparent approval to the behavior.

$ Rescuing. If you save the gambler from emotional or financial discomfort, you enable the gambling to continue.

In a return to McGurrin, and phase three, it is here where the wife finally realizes she cannot control her husbands gambling. Now she may vacillate between panic and rage.

Into phase four and she hits bottom. She feels hopeless and that she has completely lost control over her life. She may begin to abuse alcohol or prescription drugs. She may consider divorce, and frequently contemplates suicide as she sees no realistic resolution to her problems.

The study goes on to say that the effects of the pathological gambler's behavior on the children in the family are equally as significant as those impacting the spouse.

The children are reactive to both parents and many experience role conflicts. They may become scapegoats, peacemakers, or overly responsible in an attempt to restore order to the family. Unable to stabilize the family unit, these children may begin their own inappropriate acting out behaviors – common to which are inconsistent academic performance, substance abuse, overeating, delinquency, and their own gambling addiction.

As the compulsive gambler's behavior continues, the children deny and repress their anger. They feel anxious and depressed and learn to expect disappointment, failure, and tragedy in life. And, eventually, children and mother begin to look to each other to meet those needs that should be provided to them by husband and father.

In a supportive study by Wexler and Wexler, Center of Alcohol Studies - Rutgers University (n.d.), *Facts on Compulsive Gambling and Addiction*, they present a comparison of the behaviors and feelings of the pathological gambler as he progresses through his phases, as contrasted with those of the spouse as she moves through her phases in reaction to those of the gambler.

The gambler's first phase is winning. During this period he is involved in occasional gambling, he may win frequently, he displays unreasonable optimism about his skills as a gambler, and may experience a big win.

Phase one for the spouse is denial. This consists of occasional worries about the gambling behavior of the husband, but is easily reassured by him that there is no problem.

Phase two for the gambler, the losing phase, is characterized by prolonged losing episodes, covering up his behavior, lying, personality changes, a careless attitude about wife and family, and consequently an unhappy home life.

For the wife, phase two is the stress phase. Here she feels rejected. She attempts to control the husband and his gambling behavior. There are frequent arguments, and she extends herself in an attempt to borrow money to stabilize the family's financial situation.

Phase three, gambler desperation. Increased amounts of time and monies spent gambling. Alienation from family and friends, and possibly resorting to illegal acts such as theft, forgery, or embezzlement.

Phase three, spouse exhaustion. Wife is confused, doubts sanity, experiences rage, anxiety, and panic, and begins to manifest physical symptoms as a result of husband's behavior.

The final phase for the gambler is hopelessness. Here he may experience suicidal thoughts and attempts. In support of this, a study by Braniff and Trebilcock (1997) reports that 59 percent of compulsive gamblers have seriously considered suicide. Another study by Jones (1996) reports that 20 percent of compulsive gamblers seeking help have actually attempted suicide. In continuing the considerations of the gamblers final phase, he may be arrested for criminal behavior, his wife may divorce him, he may turn to abusing alcohol or other substances to ease his pain, or he may experience a total emotional break down.

The wife's final phase is helplessness. She has lost all hope. She may divorce the gambler. She may turn to alcohol or drugs for temporary relief. She may mentally breakdown, or she may consider suicide as the only option left available to her.

In a related article on effects of pathological gambling on spouses, Lorenz and Yaffee (1986) reported on the finding of their study of 215 spouses of compulsive gamblers as to their illnesses and feelings experienced during the desperation phase of their gambler husbands addiction. This being, as we have just seen in Wexler and Wexler, the exhaustion phase for the spouse.

The spouse respondents reported physical problems such as severe headaches, irritable bowels, hypertension, backaches, elevated blood pressure, and menstrual irregularities. Emotionally they were angry, resentful, depressed, lonely, and isolated from the gambler. They also felt guilt for causing or contributing to the gambling. They felt confused, ineffective as a parent as well as helpless and suicidal.

This article goes on to say that in conclusion it is not the problems resulting from the compulsive gambler's behavior that are linked to the wife's distress, but rather her emotions related to this behavior. Her coping skills are inadequate and prevent her from dealing effectively with the compulsive gambler and his maladaptive behavior.

Because of this, the spouses as well as the gamblers believe that mental health therapists must have specific training in issues related to pathological gambling in order to be effective.

CHAPTER SEVEN

Assessing the Problem

Pathological gambling is described by Blasyczynski and McConaghy (1989) as an end point on a continuum that ranges from no gambling, through to heavy and problematic gambling.

The assessment process then becomes a matter of evaluating specifics as they relate to the gambler, and determining where he falls on that continuum. For this to happen, those specifics need be defined.

In a study by DeCaria et al. (1996), they report that as a psychiatric disorder pathologic gambling may be difficult to identify and diagnose, and it is frequently overlooked in clinical settings. Essential features of pathological gambling include constantly recurring gambling behavior that is maladaptive in that personal, familial, and vocational components of the gambler's life are disrupted.

Miller (1996) calls gambling a problem when that behavior persists despite adverse consequences. He goes on to say that compounding the problem of identification of this disorder is the fact that pathological gambling has been called a hidden disease, because there are no laboratory or direct physical findings related to it.

Miller goes on to cite a study by Rosenthal and Lorenz in which they describe craving, tolerance and withdrawal as being significant features to look for in the pathological gambler when attempting to make a diagnosis.

In Walker's (1989) study of gambling addiction, he cites a study by Jacobs (1986), in which a psychological addiction could be defined as a persistent behavior pattern characterized by:

$\quad$ A desire or need to continue the activity which places it outside voluntary control.

$ A tendency to increase the frequency or amount of the activity over time.

$ A psychological dependence on the pleasurable effects of the activity.

$ A detrimental effect on the individual and society.

In Blume (1987) she states that:

Because compulsive gambling has so much in common with alcoholism and other drug addictions, and because these symptoms so often occur in the same people and families, compulsive or pathological gambling has been conceptualized as an addictive disease, reflecting the growing acceptance of an addiction model. (p. 241).

And in Rosenthal (1992) he defines pathological gambling as a progressive disorder characterized by a continuous or periodic loss of control over gambling, a preoccupation with gambling and with obtaining money with which to gamble, irrational thinking, and a continuation of the behavior despite adverse consequences. Rosenthal points out that this definition, with its emphasis on loss of control, progression, preoccupation, and disregard for consequences is similar to that for alcohol and substance dependence.

McGurrin (1992) discusses additional specifics relevant to the pathological gambler that are extremely useful considerations at time of assessment. He reports that pathological gamblers appear to vacillate between periods of extreme confidence and acute self-doubt, anxiety and depression. They tend to view delayed gratification with disregard. They have difficulty with maintaining intimate emotional relationships. Many pathological gamblers have pronounced personality traits characteristic of specific personality disorders, especially narcissistic personality disorder as well as several indicators of antisocial personality disorder. The gambler's narcissism presents as self-importance, hypersensitivity to others opinions, fragile self-esteem, and an apparent lack of empathy for those around him. The antisocial feelings are a manipulation of people by lying, failure to plan ahead and responsibly manage personal issues, difficulty with intimacy issues, impulsivity, and an inability to tolerate anxiety, boredom, or depression.

And, in a related article by Levy and Feinberg (1991), they reference Custer and Milt (1985), who suggest that people who do not have their needs of approval and affection met, who do not feel recognized, and who lack self-confidence may be predisposed to develop gambling problems.

Tasman, Kay and Lieberman (1997) indicate that it is not difficult to diagnose pathological gambling once you have the facts. They also say that it is indeed a challenge to collect those facts. Pathological gamblers view their gambling and associative behavior as egosyntonic, and as a result are inclined to lie about the extent of their involvement in this activity. The gambler may seek attention for a medical or psychological co-morbid disorder, while the gambling goes unaddressed. Some of the considerations in this area are that there is a high prevalence of additional addictive disorders in pathological gamblers, and a growing rate of prevalence of pathological gambling in those individuals experiencing alcoholism and substance abuse. And, pathological gamblers present with a high rate of affective mood disorders.

In exploring those issues of comorbidity and pathological gambling, this study found the following:

In Graham and Lowenfeld (1986), they reported that although many hypotheses have been made concerning the etiology and dynamics of pathological gambling, only limited quantitative data has been published concerning the personality characteristics of the pathological gambler.

DeCaria et al. (1996) say that "clinically, pathological gamblers may present as having affective symptomology and/or substance abuse problems since these conditions often co-occur with pathological gambling." (p. 80).

In looking first to the issue of concurrent substance abuse in pathological gamblers this study found the following evidence:

In Ciarrocchi (1987), he cites a study by McCormick et al. (1984), in which they report findings from their studies indicating that 45 percent of the pathological gamblers in their study were also substance abusers.

In Rosenthal (1991), he reports on a 1991 study by Jacobs in which seventeen hundred alcohol and drug patients in Veterans Administration Hospitals were assessed for gambling problems. Results were that 14 percent were diagnosed as pathological gamblers and another 16 percent met criteria for potential pathological gambling.

And Tasman, Kay and Lieberman (1997) report that while study done in the 1970's showed pathological gamblers with a relatively low rate of co-morbid substance abuse and dependence, about 10 percent, more current studies using better screening methods have found that rate to be from 47 percent to 52 percent, with alcohol as the most commonly abused substances.

Continuing their discussions on this issue they reported on the testing of substance abuse patients in various settings and found that between 5 percent and 25 percent of substance abusers met the criteria for pathological gambling while an additional 10 percent to 15 percent had gambling problems.

Lesieur (1992) reports that:

Systematic studies of pathological gamblers reveal rates of alcohol and other substance abuse problems ranging from 47 to 52 percent. Some research has been done on substance abusing populations to find out the extent of their problems with pathological gambling. These studies have uncovered rates of 9 to 14 percent of the patients diagnosed as pathological gamblers and 19 to 28 percent as problem or pathological gamblers. These rates are 6 to 10 times higher than for the general population. (p. 46).

And Rosenthal (1991) warns that second addictions may be simultaneous or sequential and require relevant diagnostic consideration.

In the area of additional comorbidity issues experienced by pathological gamblers this study found that in DeCaria et al. (1996) they reported that among those patients in their study that were hospitalized for pathological gambling problems, 76 percent met criteria for major depressive disorder, and 38 percent were hypomanic. Among their outpatient sample, 28 percent met criteria for major depressive disorder while 24 percent had bipolar disorder and 28 percent had anxiety disorders.

De Caria et al. go on to cite a study by Custer and Milt (1985) in which they report that the tendency to be depressed and anxious was part of the personality structure of the compulsive gambler in his youth and early adult life, even before the gambling became an addiction. And the depression was manifested in sullenness, moodiness, and isolation or withdrawal.

An additional study cited in this article is one by Murray (1993) in which it is stated that:

Depression appears to coexist frequently with compulsive gambling, but the antecedent - consequent relationship is unclear and both conditions may form part of a larger personality disorder as yet uncategorized (p. 798).

DeCaria et al. go on to say that other researchers have suggested that compulsive gambling can be seen as an attempt to ward off a severe or impending depression. And, they cite Boyd and Bolen (1970) as considering gambling as a manic defense against helplessness and depression secondary to loss.

In Blasycyzinki and McConaghy (1994), they report on findings of their study of the prevalence of antisocial personality disorder and its relationship to criminal offenses in pathological gamblers. Those findings being that the features of an antisocial personality emerged in response to attempts to hide gambling and related financial issues from significant others. Needing to chase losses, this behavior depleted legal sources of funding and consequently illegal behaviors became the only option left available to the gambler.

And, Glazer (1996) reports that pathological gambling can enhance stress-related diseases as well as psychiatric problems. This position is supported by Miller (1996), in which he reports his patients reporting with gambling induced conditions such as dyspepsia, diarrhea, headaches, low back pain, dermatitis, hypertension, and chest pain in addition to depression, anxiety, and substance abuse.

In a closing look at the comorbidity issues, Tasman, Kay and Lieberman (1997) present the following information:

In several surveys, between 70 and 80 percent of pathological gamblers also met the criteria for a major depressive episode, a manic episode, or a hypomanic episode at some point in their life. More than 50 percent had recurrent major depressive episodes. And between 32 percent and 46 percent of these patients met criteria for bipolar disorder, bipolar II disorder, or cyclothymic disorder.

Between 12 and 24 percent of pathological gambling patients had a history of at least one suicide attempt related to their addiction, with one study reporting that 80 percent of those patients surveyed had a history of either suicide attempts or suicidal ideation. Additionally, these studies showed that the prevalence of obsessive compulsive disorder, panic disorder, generalized anxiety disorder, and eating disorders were significantly higher in the pathological gamblers than in the general population. And, they present a greater prevalence of stress-related medical conditions, such as peptic ulcer disease, hypertension, and migraine headaches.

In a return to DeCaria et al. (1996), they say that compulsive gambling has severely impacted the lives of its participants and that the multiple comorbidity issues such as substance abuse, affective disorders, personality disorders, and physical concerns have greatly complicated the gambler's clinical profile.

In consideration of the formulation of that clinical profile, the following nine criteria have been set forth by Rosenthal (1991).

1.   DSM-IV Diagnostic criteria.
     A.   Persistent and recurrent maladaptive gambling behavior
                 as indicated by five (or more) of the following:

    $ Is preoccupied with gambling (e.g., preoccupied with reliving past gambling experiences, handicapping or planning the next venture, or thinking of ways to get money with which to gamble).

    $ Needs to gamble with increasing amounts of money in order to achieve the desired excitement.

    $ Has repeated unsuccessful efforts to control, cut back, or stop gambling.

    $ Is restless or irritable when attempting to cut down or stop gambling.

    $ Gambles as a way of escaping from problems or of relieving a dysphoric mood (e.g., feelings of helplessness, guilt, anxiety, depression).

    $ After losing money gambling, often returns another day to get even (chasing ones losses).

    $ Lies to family members, therapist, or others to conceal the extent of involvement with gambling.

    $ Has committed illegal acts such as forgery, fraud, theft, or embezzlement to finance gambling.

    $ Has jeopardized or lost a significant relationship, job, or educational or career opportunity because of gambling.

    $ Relies on others to provide money to relieve a desperate financial situation caused by gambling.

  B. The gambling behavior is not better accounted for by a manic episode.

2. Determine the severity of the problem.
3. Identify coexisting mental/physical disorders.
4. Gather gambling history including precipitating and progression factors.
5. Develop a psychological portrait including coping style, defenses, strengths, and weaknesses.
6. Explore significant reality factors.
7. Establish baseline determinations for subsequent evaluation.
8. Develop a psychodynamic formulation.
9. Develop a treatment plan.

It is at this point where the advice of McGurrin (1992) plays a significant role. There are no experts in this field and clinicians working with pathological gamblers need to value their own observations and insights.

In collecting data for purpose of diagnosis, the clinician may rely primarily on three sources, the pathological gambler, a collateral (i.e., spouse, etc.), and relevant testing.

As to the first of these, the gambler, Pasternak (1997) reports that this information is unreliable. Even if there is a problem they tend to deny its existence. Here Pasternak suggests that perhaps an indirect method of questioning with the gambler may prove to be more effective. And, Blasyczynski and McConaghy (1994) indicate that when confronted with their behavior, pathological gamblers may exhibit characteristics of an antisocial personality disorder in an attempt to conceal their gambling activity and related behaviors.

As to the collateral interview with spouse or significant other, Miller (1996) is recalled along with his referral to pathological gambling as the "hidden disease," because of its lack of obvious signs and symptoms. Because of this, collateral information may be primarily relevant to the impact of the gambler's behavior on that individual and they may be unable to provide specific information as relates to the gambler simply because they are not aware.

The final source for information comes from testing. These are primarily the self-report, gambling-specific questionnaires, and specific psychological tests as deemed necessary and/or appropriate.

As to the gambling-specific questionnaires, there are currently two in common use. One is the Gamblers Anonymous Twenty Questions, described by McGurrin (1992) as a supportive supplement to the DSM-III-R diagnostic criteria and useful in evaluating control issues relating to gambling behaviors. Affirmative responses to any combination of four or more of the questions is a reliable indicator of problem gambling.

The other instrument of this type is the South Oaks Gambling Screen (SOGS) described by Pasternak (1997) as a standardized instrument used for the assessment of pathological gambling. A panel of twenty questions incorporates concepts for the DSM-III as well as the twenty questions used by Gamblers Anonymous to evaluate problem gambling. A score of three to four on the SOGS indicates a problem gambler, while a score of five or higher indicates a pathological gambling pattern.

The South Oaks Gambling Screen is called by Glazer (1998) "currently the only one reliable, validated screening instrument that can identify pathological gamblers" (p. 75).

Volberg and Banks (1990) report that they found that the sensitivity of the South Oaks Gambling Screen in its ability to correctly detect pathological gamblers was extremely high when administered to members of Gamblers Anonymous, a finding of 99.5 percent. The specificity of SOGS, or its ability to not falsely detect pathological gambling, was also extremely high when administered to groups of non-gamblers, with results of 98.5 percent to 99.3 percent.

The final testing option, the psychological testing, is again arbitrary. It may or may not be necessary depending on the individual case. In an article by Becona, Lorenzi and Fuentes (1996), they report that a number of studies have found that pathological gamblers tend to obtain high scores on the depression and psychopathic deviation scales of the Minnesota Multiphasic Personality Inventory (Glen, 1979; Graham and Lowerfeld, 1986; McCormick and Taber, 1988; Moravec and Munley, 1983). They go on to say that similar results have been obtained by those who have evaluated depression with the Beck Depression Inventory (Blasyczynski, McConaghy and Frankova, 1990), the Schedule of Affective Disorders (McCormick, Russo, Ramirey and Taber, 1984), and the Symptom Check list 90 (Blasyczynski and McConaghy, 1988). This then represents completion of resources for data collection to answer Rosenthal's (1991) nine criteria for clinical profiling and an ultimate determination of location on the gambling continuum as described by Blasyczynski and McConaghy (1989).

CHAPTER EIGHT

Treatment

A review of current research has provided the following observations relevant to considerations surrounding the treatment of pathological gambling.

In Shaffer (1986), he is of the opinion that:

The study of compulsive gambling is a field in conceptual crisis. The field is in a stage of development that lacks guidelines necessary to focus theory and instruct research. Assertions in the field lack fact status. Diverse explanations of excessive gambling coexist with little opportunity for confrontation and disconfirmation. Without the conceptual support obtained by the resolution of this scientific crisis, all available evidence can seem equally important. Scientific confusion and frustration often can result. (p. 3).

Then, Ciarrocchi and Richardson (1989) make the following observation:

Our empirical knowledge about the treatment of pathological gambling currently comes from studies of surveys and observation of pathological gamblers through their self-help organizations. To date, the bulk of literature in the treatment field has been dominated by theoretical and non-empirical studies which, though normative in the early stages of a new field's development, tend to weaken the generalizability of information across treatment settings and different populations. (p. 53 - 54).

And, in an article supporting the position of these previous two, Blasyczynski and Silove (1995), nine years later, report that in their findings:

To date, there is no comprehensive model of gambling available that effectively explains the pathogenic process grading to the transition from controlled to pathological gambling. This absence of a unifying theory is reflected in the divergence of approaches to management and treatment of pathological gambling, ranging from specific individual techniques to broad-based multimodal packages. (p. 196).

In addition to a lack of understanding of cause, and a unified approach to treatment, there are additional problems in this area.

In Ladoucer, Sylvain, Letarte, Giloux and Jacques (1998), they report that "few treatment programs have been developed to help pathological gamblers and controlled studies are rare" (p. 1112).

Burke (1996) reports that in the United States there are less than 12 inpatient and 100 outpatient facilities to treat pathological gamblers.

And, Miller (1996) reports that "treatment services are in under supply due partly to structural deficiencies in reimbursement for treatment in the current medical economic environment." (p. 633).

Compounding the problem, in a related article by Miller (1996), he states that "there are not many clinicians who have developed special expertise in the treatment of pathological gambling" (p. 638). And, Estes and Brubaker (1994) report on their research which indicates that only a handful of clinicians in the United States are skilled in the diagnosis and treatment of pathological gambling.

Yet, even with these issues of theoretical shortcomings, a lack of treatment programs as well as trained personnel, we are told by Rosenthal (1992) that "in the hands of an experienced therapist, pathological gambling is an extremely treatable disorder" (p. 5).

After consideration of all the data collected during the assessment phase, the diagnosis of the gambler, or where he is placed on the gambling continuum, becomes all important. If the findings are of pathological gambling, and there is a recommendation for treatment, there are two modalities available.

One is inpatient hospitalization, where the gambler actually becomes institutionalized for a period of time, and the other is outpatient treatment, which allows the gambler to continue in his current social vocational environment while pursuing a course of treatment.

A determination of which treatment option is appropriate for the gambler is based on presenting symptomology. Rosenthal (1991) indicates that for inpatient hospitalization, the following criteria should be considered:

$ The gambler is unable to stop gambling and has had previously failed attempts at outpatient treatment.

$ The gambler exhibits signs of severe comorbidity issues including multiple addictions.

$ The gambler has no obvious support system.

$ The gambler shows signs of extreme physical or emotional exhaustion.

$ The gambler has a history of suicide attempts and/or currently entertains thoughts of harming himself or others.

However, even though many pathological gamblers meet some, or indeed all of these criteria, the inpatient option of treatment may be unavailable to them. Previously cited information in this study has addressed this concern. Burke (1996) reported that there are less than 12 inpatient treatment centers for pathological gambling in the United States.

And, on a practical side, Miller (1996) reports that it is usually at the end stages of their addiction when the pathological gambler acknowledges a need for professional help. By this time there are no financial resources available for treatment. However, Miller goes on to present an option for consideration. He quotes a representative of the Blue Cross/Blue Shield health care programs as saying, "Compulsive gambling, in and of itself, is not considered a primary diagnosis in terms of payment for treatment. But if gambling results in a health issue, say acute depression, then it's covered" (p. 638).

In the absence of diagnostic criteria indicating inpatient treatment, the gambler is referred to outpatient services. In this treatment modality, unlike inpatient hospitalization, the gambler attempts to participate in, and concentrate on, their recovery while continuing on the job, if employed, staying in the family system, if intact, as well as facing the daily pressures and temptations of life.

This treatment alternative presents both positives and negatives to the gambler. On the plus side, it is less disruptive to a lifestyle, it may allow for easier access to treatment and it is less costly than inpatient services. The downside of this option would be that it may be extremely difficult for the gambler to continue all existing behaviors except one, the gambling, and, it may be difficult on the family wondering when or if the gambler may revert to old behavior patterns.

Once established in a treatment modality, the goals of the pathological gambler, as described by Tasman, Kay and Lieberman (1997), are abstinence from gambling, rehabilitation of the family and work roles and relationships, treatment of co-morbid disorders and relapse prevention. An article by Blume (1995) indicates that treatment for pathological gambling consists of a combination of professional and self-help, and that long-term follow-up is essential.

In returning to Tasman, Kay and Lieberman (1997), they describe treatment consisting of individual therapy, family therapy, treatment of co-morbid disorders, medication treatment, and participation in a self-help organization, Gamblers Anonymous.

In their description of this organization, combined with observations from Walker (1993), Gamblers Anonymous can best be described as follows:

Gamblers Anonymous is a mutual support group, based on peer relationships, that encourages its members to admit their inability to stop gambling and attempt to take control of their lives. The view of this group is that pathological gambling is a progressive disease and that those suffering from this affliction cannot gamble. To accomplish this, they encourage their membership to focus on abstinence one day at a time. For many in recovery, this disease concept is most helpful in assisting them in dealing with their guilt and their shame. It also helps them to see that they are not unique in their addiction, that there are others experiencing similar problems, and as a result they are able to learn from some as well as be a help to others.

Additionally, participation in this group allows for a base of social interaction where the recovering gambler can meet others sharing similar experiences, and can, perhaps, establish new friendships that are in keeping with his new life style.

Of note is that Gamblers Anonymous may not be suited for everyone in recovery. Some individuals simply find the group experience not to their liking, and Rosenthal (1992) reports that only 2 percent to 4 percent of the members of Gamblers Anonymous are women, and that this under representation is assumed to be related to the perception of social stigma as relates to females and pathological gambling.

Tasman, Kay and Liberman indicate that individual therapy is considered necessary in conjunction with self-help. They recommend individual therapy because they feel many gamblers need to understand why they gamble. This therapy should involve the confronting and teasing out the vicissitudes of the patient's sense of omnipotence, dealing with the self-deceptions and defensive aspects of the gambler's lying, boundary issues, and problems related to magical thinking and reality, and, attention to relapse prevention.

Family therapy is essential for an opportunity for the gambler to make amends, learn communication skills, and deal with intimacy problems. This is also an opportunity to see what, if any, problems that family members are experiencing as a result of the gambler's behavior.

This article goes on to say that any co-morbid disorders need to be identified and treated. These consist of mostly addictive and affective disorders and may require hospitalization for treatment before the pathological gambling issues can be addressed.

And finally, even though this article reports that medication treatment of pathological gambling is understudied, they indicate that because cessation of gambling is often associated with a major depressive episode, prophylactic use of an antidepressant may be warranted even in the absence of a preexisting depressive episode.

In an exploration of methods used to address the aforementioned treatment goals, this study turned its attention to Walker (1993) for explanation and description.

Group Psychotherapy provides opportunity to learn and practice the rewards of responsibility, acceptance, patience, self-discipline, and sensitivity. It uses the group process to bring about change in behavior and possibly change in the personality of the group members. It allows patients to confront one another about undesirable behavior, and change usually comes about because the gambler is too insecure to stand up to group pressure and censure. Group Psychotherapy is frequently complemented by individual and marital therapy, as well as educational programs on addiction.

In consideration of *Conjoint Marital Therapy*, Walker states that the rationale for this approach notes that the pathological gambling is often used as a defense against the stresses threatening the marriage. The symptoms of pathological gambling must be understood in the larger context of an even more complicated marital symptom and interaction complex. The therapy must allow both partners to become less defensive and to face the problems in the relationship.

In looking at *Psychoanalysis* and the pathological gambler, this behavior is seen as but one of a long series of unconsciously self-provoked, self-created, self-perpetuated, and self-damaging tragedies in their life. Walker cites an article by Bergler (1957) in which he says:

The important aspect of gambling for the compulsive gambler is the losing and the consequences that follow from losing. Every compulsive gambler gambles for masochistic reasons. All of the overt reasons given by the gambler can be shown to be false: If one is gambling to win, then why continue when losing; and if one is gambling for the excitement or as an escape, then why do it at such a cost? (p. 541).

So, psychoanalytic therapy attempts to uncover the real reasons for the gambling behavior and to show that the gambler's conscious thoughts about gambling are a cover for more significant issues.

Aversion Therapy refers to a type of intervention that produces a negative response when an undesired behavior is exhibited. In the treatment of pathological gambling, usually the gambling behavior is paired with an electric shock. Repeated pairings diminish the pleasure associated with gambling and induce anxiety when the gambling behavior is initiated.

Behavioral Counseling is where the therapist, gambler, and significant others in the gambler's life cooperate to construct a plan for a behavioral change by the gambler. Usually of the type that the gambling is replaced by other enjoyable activities, perhaps new, or reintroduced to those previously pursued before the gambling took over his life. Positive reinforcement for embracing and continuing these behavioral changes are significant to the effectiveness of this project.

In examining *Cognitive-Based Treatment Strategies*, one type of therapy is referred to as thought stopping. It is believed that the urge to gamble is experienced as thoughts about gambling and gambling behavior follows from the intention to gamble expressed in thoughts. Cognitive therapies attempt to modify those thought patterns so that undesirable behavior is not triggered. In the treatment of pathological gambling, the patient is instructed to monitor his impulse to gamble. When thoughts of gambling are detected, a thought stopping or replacement technique is instigated. Perhaps a rubber band on the wrist is snapped, patient says stop out loud, and this redirects thought and subsequently behavior.

A second cognitive strategy is cognitive restructuring. Walker refers to (Baucum, 1985, p. 201) and his contention that "much of what passes for pathology in gambling is relatively straightforward, mistaken belief that it is possible to win consistently even in games of pure chance." Thus, cognitive restructuring assumes that gambling is maintained by irrational thinking and treatment should focus on changing the irrational beliefs to those more consistent with the reality of gambling.

And in a final look at treatment methods, this study explores Miller (1986) and his *Four-Phase Approach* to the problem of pathological gambling.

Miller's view of this issue is that gambling provides the gambler with action, a method of dealing with stress, and avoiding unpleasant effects, as well as a variety of social, psychological, and existential benefits. And recovery from pathological gambling is viewed as a process whereby the pathological gambler chooses to lose an addiction to gambling and maintains that choice while mourning the loss of gambling. This loss of gambling is seen as a complicated and significant one that elicits grief responses similar to those seen in response to other types of major loss. And the role of the clinician is to help the recovering gambler accept his loss and learn to live without it.

Miller defines his specific grief responses as denial, bargaining, hope, sadness, guilt, anger, and acceptance. In looking at each of these individually and in relation to their role in the interaction with the pathological gambler, there are the following considerations:

Denial: The pathological gambler denies or minimizes the connection between gambling and his problems, and he denies or minimizes his lack of control over gambling.

Bargaining: This is indicative of some advance over gross denial because it is here where the pathological gambler consciously admits that something should be done about the gambling.

Hope: Here the gambler sees some of the benefits of life without gambling, and this hope that things will improve helps provide motivation through recovery.

Sadness: This is the realization that everything lost by gambling, as well as the activity of gambling itself, is lost forever.

Guilt: The gambler feels responsible for all he has done or not done as the case may be, in regards to his gambling and associated behaviors.

Anger: Associated with loss, anger may be directed at anyone: other gamblers, family, therapist.

Acceptance: The gambler realizes that he lacks control over gambling and it has made his life unmanageable.

Miller sees these reactions of the pathological gambler as being processed through what he calls phases of treatment that correspond to the exhibited grief reactions in response to the chosen goal of abstinence.

The first phase of treatment is working with those compulsive gamblers who have not yet made a commitment to abstinence; denial. The second phase requires the gambler to identify and confront the problems that have been caused by gambling, while making an attempt to stop gambling but still not strongly committed to a life of abstinence; bargaining, hope. Phase three is where the gambler's commitment is strengthening and he is working through later stages of mourning and acceptance and focusing on longer term problems; sadness, guilt and anger. And the final phase involves those who have accepted that they must not gamble again but cannot quite yet see themselves in a life without gambling; acceptance.

Even as this information describes the process experienced by the gambler as he progresses through treatment, there is no specific dictate as to what type of treatment approach is to be used. That is an individual determination to be made by the clinician based on his experience and training, as well as the background, need, and therapeutic capacities of the pathological gambler. Those determinations become the clinical components for consideration in the pathological gambler's treatment plans.

That treatment plan is a positive reactive proposal to the presenting problems of the individual. It is a practical plan for recovery that specifically outlines the goals of treatment.

Primary to treatment considerations is abstinence. Rosenthal and Rugle (1994) report that the five strategies to employ with the pathological gambler in an attempt to achieve abstinence are: (1) breaking through the denial; (2) confronting omnipotent defenses; (3) interrupting the chasing cycle; (4) identifying reasons for gambling; and (5) motivating the patient to become an active participant in treatment. In Miller (1996), treatment plan recommendations include:

$ Behavioral changes: stop gambling, discontinue other inappropriate behaviors, develop healthy behaviors
$ Biological changes: develop sense of responsibility for wellness, initiate healthy activities (i.e., diet, exercise)
$ Cognitive changes: Increase awareness of disorder, recognize and decrease denial
$ Affective changes: Manage anxiety and depression, increase ability to tolerate feelings without defenses, manage shame and guilt, take pride in the recovery process that builds self-esteem.
$ Social changes: make amends for inappropriate behaviors, reconnect with family, increase personal responsibility including legal and financial obligations as necessary.
$ Spiritual changes: re-establish personal values and accept self.

And, the final component of the treatment plan is attention to relapse prevention. In Blasyczynski and Sicove (1995), they say that "once the drive, urge, and preoccupation to gamble is reduced, steps must be taken to address the issue of avoiding high-risk situations and minimizing risk for relapse." (p. 213). Here the pathological gambler should identify all potential cues, triggers, and behaviors that could ultimately precipitate relapse.

However, regardless of how cautious, careful, and committed the gambler may be to his recovery, relapse may occur. If so, this behavior should not be seen as unusual. The gambler will feel guilt and shame, but should not use these negative emotions as a reason to continue inappropriate behaviors. Relapse should provide instead a lesson. A lesson of the power of the addiction. The precipitators should be analyzed and appropriate remedial measures incorporated into the treatment plan in an effort to avoid future similar behaviors.

In looking at the prognosis of those individuals suffering from pathological gambling disorder, we are told by Tasman, Kay and Lieberman (1997) that without treatment, the prognosis is poor. It runs a chronic course with increasing morbidity and comorbidity, disruption of family and work roles and relationships, increasing financial difficulties, potential criminal involvement, and possible suicide attempts. But, in the care of an experienced clinician it is an extremely treatable disorder with a favorable prognosis.

The study goes on to say that the difference between a poor and a good prognosis depends on treatment, and treatment depends on an accurate diagnosis.

In support of this favorable prognosis position, The Harvard Mental Health Letter (January 1996) reports that "30 to 70 percent of patients who start a course of treatment for pathological gambling complete it, and 20 to 50 percent are no longer gambling a year later." (p. 5). And Pasternak (1997) reports that early studies have shown success rates in the treatment of pathological gambling to be greater than 50 percent. This word success is one that is frequently employed and as frequently misunderstood when used in conjunction with this disorder. There are currently no clearly defined criteria for measuring success other than that abstention of the undesirable behavior equals success.

In Rosenthal (1991), he says that as state and local governments turn more and more to legalized gambling to increase revenues without having to raise taxes, we can expect to see a greater incidence of problem and pathological gambling. And, the clinician should anticipate the need to know more about this disorder.

CHAPTER NINE

Discussion

For many people gambling is an exciting and enjoyable activity with no adverse effects on their finances, work, or family relationships. However, for some, gambling becomes seriously maladaptive and results in a multiplicity of lifestyle problems. This type of maladaptive behavior is referred to as pathological gambling.

It has been called by Mobilia (1993) "America's latest social addiction" (p. 122). And, currently affecting 10 to 12 million Americans.

Research and theory cited in this study has shown that pathological gambling is a sizeable and significant problem in today's society.

It has shown that state and local governments, in an attempt to avoid introduction of new taxes, have hastily and perhaps with limited foresight legalized gambling activities in their communities without the realization of the potential problems it may cause.

This study has offered the diagnosis of pathological gambling as set forth in the Diagnostic and Statistical Manual of Mental Disorders, Fourth Edition. It has also cited evidence that in spite of this diagnosis, there is an obvious lack of agreement of definition of pathological gamblers by researchers and practitioners in the field.

This is reflected in an article by McGurrin (1992, p. 9), in which he reports that "although research has thus far found evidence of cognitive (Corney and Cummings, 1985), affective (McCormick et al. 1984), and physiological (Carlton and Goldstein, 1987; Carlton and Manowitz, 1988), dimensions to pathological gambling, a precise and definitive formulation of the personality structure and psychodynamics of the pathological gambler has not yet been developed (Jaber, 1988)."

Combined with this lack of agreement is another as relates to the field of treatment for this disorder. Existing research shows little or no empirical evidence as relates to treatment methods and/or effectiveness.

Even though treatment for this disorder began in the 1960's, as reported by Pasternak (1997), it was not recognized until 1980 when it was listed in the Diagnostic and statistical Manual of Mental Disorders, Third Edition. Even having been a recognized disorder for 20 years, and treated as such for 30-plus years, Miller (1996) reports that this population is greatly underserved due to a lack of treatment facilities, as well as a limited number of knowledgeable practitioners.

However, even in spite of these issues, Rosenthal (1992) says that pathological gambling is a treatable disorder. This claim is supported by Pasternak (1997), citing studies showing success rates in the treatment of pathological gambling in excess of 50 percent.

That then was the purpose of this book. To explore current research and theory in an attempt to answer the question: Is pathological gambling a treatable disorder? And, if so, what are the necessary considerations for helping professionals who treat clients with pathological gambling disorders?

This study answered that question through use of available research and theory and provided an overview of the problem, both historical and current. It provided a familiarization with the activity of gambling. It identified and explained who the gamblers are. It detailed specifics in order to differentiate between problem/pathological gambling and normal gambling behavior. It looked at the effects of the disorder on the gambler, as well as those around him, family, etc. It explored significant factors in consideration of problem assessment. It provided information regarding treatment modalities and methods. It detailed elements to be included in a patient treatment plan for the most comprehensive attention to the disorder possible. And, it encouraged clinicians to trust their abilities, knowledge and experience, while always maintaining an open mind in an attempt to increase their understanding of this disorder.

In that regard, the following researchers have made observations/recommendations that they feel would contribute to the understanding and treatment of pathological gambling.

Lesieur (1992) proposes the following:
- $ No new forms of gambling should be legalized by local governments without first providing for treatment on demand of all gambling related problems, with all costs for treatment coming from gambling revenues.
- $ No promotion of gambling should be allowed without a warning label and an 800 number to call for help with gambling problems.

$ Epidemiological studies of all gamblers should be conducted to learn what percentage of the monies being wagered comes from problem gamblers.

$ A percentage of revenues should be directed to education, research, and treatment of pathological gambling disorder.

Glazer (1997) sees research needs in the following areas:

$ Education of the medical profession regarding pathological gambling.

$ Whether or not abstinence is the only goal for this disorder, or is controlled gambling a realistic possibility.

$ And, how can there be more programs developed to make treatment for this disorder more widely available.

The National Gambling Impact Study Commission Report (1999) found that "government and private-sector efforts to treat gambling addiction have been inadequate, leaving the addiction field without a proven treatment approach for problem gamblers." (p. 2).

As a result, they have made the following recommendations for prevention and better treatment of pathological gambling:

$ State gambling taxes should be dedicated toward pathological gambling research, treatment, prevention, and education.

$ States should conduct biennial surveys on problem prevalence.

$ States should develop outcome measures for various treatment methods.

$ States should maintain a list of professional treatment centers.

$ States should mandate that insurance companies and managed care providers identify successful treatment programs and cover appropriate programs under their plans.

$ Each state approved gambling operation post telephone numbers of problem gambling treatment providers as well as referral information.

$ State should require that gambling facilities contract with a state-recognized professional to train staff in identification of problem gamblers.

In Spunt, Dupont, Lesieur, Liberty and Hunt (1998), they recommend research considerations into the area of:

$ The relationship between pathological gambling and substances such as alcohol, heroin, and cocaine.

$ And a pursuit of additional knowledge about female gamblers, especially those with substance abuse problems.

And finally, McGurrin (1992) presents a list of concerns relevant to the field that require research and, hopefully, clarification:

$ Is pathological gambling an impulse disorder, an addictive disorder, a personality disorder, or an obsessive compulsive disorder?

$ Should pathological gambling be viewed as a disease, a conditioned response, or an existential disorder?

$ Is the risk of becoming a pathological gambler equal for all persons, or are there predisposing genetic familial factors that place some persons at higher risk?

$ Can pathological gamblers be cured and eventually engage in normal gambling activity?

$ Are peer counselors more effective at treating other pathological gamblers?

$ Can pathological gamblers benefit from treatment before their gambling hits a crisis stage?

$ How effective are the different approaches to treating pathological gambling?

$ What are the prodomal signs of relapse, and can relapse be effectively prevented?

$ Are there differential incidences and prevalence rates related to age, sex, race, and family history, or do differences result from measurement errors?

$ Is incidence and prevalence casually related to gambling opportunities? And is legalization and regulation increasing the numbers of pathological gamblers?

$ Are some forms of gambling more likely than others to cause pathological gambling?

$ Are pathological gamblers motivated by the possibility of winning money, or do they seek a special emotional experience called the action?

McGurrin goes on to say:

> The knowledge and treatment of pathological gambling undoubtedly will be modified many times before it stabilizes on a well-tested scientific foundation. In the meantime, pathological gambling exists and is apparently growing in prevalence. The practitioner, therefore, must provide treatment now based on the best knowledge available. (p. IX).

To provide that knowledge was the focus of this study, to explore current theory, research, and method in the hope of providing a better understanding of, and a more effective treatment approach for those practitioners treating those persons experiencing the consequences of pathological gambling.

Bibliography

Aasved, Mikal J., & Laundergan, J. Clark (Winter 1993). Gambling and its impacts in a northeastern Minnesota community: an exploratory study. *Journal of Gambling Studies 9*(4), 301-319.

Abbot, Maree, Palmisso, Barbara & Dickerson, Mark (Fall 1995). Video game playing, dependency and delinquency: a question of methodology? *Journal of Gambling Studies 11*(3), 287-301.

Abbott, Douglas A. & Cramer, Sheran L. (Fall 1993). Gambling attitudes and participation: a Midwestern survey. *Journal of Gambling Studies 9*(3), 247263.

Abt, Vicki & McGurrin, Martin C. (Winter 1992). Commercial gambling and values in American society: the social construction of risk. *Journal of Gambling Studies 8*(4), 413-419.

Adkins, Bonnie J. (Fall 1988). Discharge planning with pathological gamblers: an ongoing process. *Journal of Gambling Behavior 4*(3), 208-218.

Anderson, G,. Brown, R. & Iain, F. (Fall 1987). Some applications of reversal theory to the explanation of gambling and gambling addictions. *Journal of Gambling Behavior 3*(3), 180-189.

Ashley, Leonard R.N. (Fall 1990). The words of my mouth, and the meditation of my heart: the mind set of gamblers revealed in their language. *Journal of Gambling Studies 6*(3), 241-259.

Barnes, Grace M., Welte, John W., Hoffman, Joseph H., & Sintcheff, Barbara A. (1999). Gambling and alcohol use among youth: influences of demographic, socialization, and individual factors. *Addictive Behaviors 24*(6), 749-767.

Becona, Elisardo, Lorenzi, Maria Del Carmen, & Fuentes, Maria Jose (1996). Pathological gambling and depression. *Psychological Reports 78*, 635-640.

Berman, L., & Siegel, M. (1992). *Behind the Eight Ball.* New York: Simon and Schuster.

Bissell, L., & Royce, J. (1987). *Ethics For Addiction Professionals.* Hazelden Publications.

Black, Spencer (1996, September). Wisconsin must act on compulsive gambling. *Wisconsin Medical Journal 96*(9), 608-609.

Blasyczynski, Alex P. (1999). Pathological gambling and obsessive-compulsive spectrum disorders. *Psychological Reports 84*, 107-113.

Blasyczynski, Alex P., & McConaghy, Neil (1989, Spring). The medical model of pathological gambling: current shortcomings. *Journal of Gambling Behavior 5*(1), 43-51.

Blasyczynski, Alex P., & McConaghy, Neil (1993). A two- to nine-year treatment follow-up study of pathological gambling. *Publications of the Gamblers Studies Series of the University of Nevada Press.*

Blasyczynski, Alex P., & McConaghy, Neil (1994, Summer). Antisocial personality disorder and pathological gambling. *Journal of Gambling Studies 10*(2), 129145.

Blasyczynski, Alex P., & Silove, Derrick (1995, Summer). Cognitive and behavioral therapies for pathological gambling. *Journal of Gambling Studies 11*(2), 195217.

Blasyczynski, Alex P., McConaghy, Neil, & Frankova, Anna (1989, Summer). Crime, antisocial personality, and pathological gambling. *Journal of Gambling Behavior 5*(2), 137-151.

Blume, A. (August 26, 1995). Pathological gambling: an addiction to an altered psychological state. *British Medical Journal.*

Blume, Sheila B. (1987, Winter). Compulsive gambling and the medical model. *Journal of Gambling Behavior 3*(4), 237-247.

Blume, Sheila B. (1994, Spring). Pathological gambling and switching addictions. Report of a case. *Journal of Gambling Studies 10*(1).

Braidfoot, Larry (1988, Winter). Legalization of lotteries in the 1980s. *Journal of Gambling Behavior 4*(4), 282-289.

Braniff, Brenda, & Trebilcock, Bob (1997, June). My husband's secret addiction. (gambling addiction) (includes related information on helping a spouse with a gambling addiction). *Good Housekeeping 224*(6) 92(4).

Brenner, Gabrielle A., & Brenner, Reuven (1990, Winter). Gambling: the shaping of an opinion. *Journal of Gambling Studies 6*(4), 297-311.

Brown, Basil R. (1991). The selective adaptation of the alcoholics anonymous program by gamblers anonymous. *Journal of Gambling Studies 7*(3), 187-206.

Brown, R., & F. Iain (1993). *Some Contributions of the Study of Gambling to the Study of Other Addictions*. Publications of the Gambling Studies of the University of Nevada Press.

Brown, R. & Iain, F. (1987, Summer). Pathological gambling and associated patterns of crime: comparisons with alcohol and other drug addictions. *Journal of Gambling Behavior 3*(2), 98-113.

Brown, R. & Iain, F. (1987, Winter). Models of gambling and gambling addictions as perceptual filters. *Journal of Gambling Behavior 3*(4), 224-235.

Burke, Judith D. (1996, September 1996). Problem gambling hits home. *Wisconsin Medical Journal 96*(9), 611-617.

Bybee, Shannon (1988, Winter). Problem gambling: one view from the gaming industry side. *Journal of Gambling Behavior 4*(4), 301-308.

Carlton, Peter L., & Manowitz, Paul (1987, Winter). Physiological factors as determinants of pathological gambling. *Journal of Gambling Behavior 3*(4), 274-285.

Carlton, Peter L., & Manowitz, Paul (1994, Summer). Factors determining the severity of pathological gambling in males. *Journal of Gambling Studies 10*(2), 147-157.

Castellani, Brian, & Rugle, Loreen (1995). A Comparison of pathological gamblers to alcoholics and cocaine misusers on impulsivity, sensation seeking, and craving. *The International Journal of the Addictions 30*(3), 275-289.

Ciarrocchi, Joseph W. (1987, Spring). Severity of impairment in dually addicted gamblers. *Journal of Gambling Behavior 3*(1), 16-25.

Ciarrocchi, Joseph W. (1993, Fall). Rates of pathological gambling in publicly funded outpatient substance abuse treatment. *Journal of Gambling Studies* 9(3), 289-293.

Ciarrocchi, Joseph W., & Richardson, Richard (1989, Spring). Profile of compulsive gamblers in treatment: update and comparisons. *Journal of Gambling Behavior* 5(1), 53-65.

Ciarrocchi, Joseph W., Kirschner, Neil M., & Fallik, Fred (1991, Summer). Personality dimensions of male pathological gamblers, alcoholics, and dually addicted gamblers. *Journal of Gambling Studies* 7(2), 133-141.

Commission finds lack of efforts to treat gambling addiction. (June 28, 1999). *Alcoholism and Drug Abuse Weekly* 11(26), 1.

Compulsive gambling may be inherited (1999, April). *USA Today Magazine* 127(2647), 7 (1).

Coventry, Kenny R., Brown, R., & Iain, F. (1993). Sensation seeking in gamblers and non-gamblers and its relation to preference for gambling activities, chasing, arousal and loss of control in regular gamblers. *Addiction.* The Society for the Study of Addiction.

Cummings, Theodore W., & Corney, William (1987, Fall). A conceptual model of gambling behavior: Fishbein's theory of reasoned action. *Journal of Gambling Behavior* 3(3), 190-201.

Cummings, Thomas N. & Gambino, Blase (1992, Winter). Perceptions by treatment staff of critical tasks in the treatment of the compulsive gambler. *Journal of Gambling Studies* 8(2), 181-199.

Cunningham-Williams, Renee M., Cottler, Linda B., Compton III, Wilson M., & Spitznagel, Edward L. (1998, July). Taking chances: problem gamblers and mental health disorders results from the st. Louis epidemiologic catchment area study. *American Journal of Public Health* 88(7), 1093-1095.

Cusak, John R., Malaney, Kathleen R., & DePry, Dennis L. (1993, April). Insights about pathological gamblers: Achasing losses" in spite of the consequences. *Postgraduate Medicine* 93(5), 169-177.

Custer, R.L., & Milt, H. (1985). When luck runs out: help for compulsive gamblers and their families. *Facts on File Publications.* New York.

Dandurand, Lawrence (1990, Spring). Market niche analysis in the casino gaming industry. *Journal of Gambling Studies 6*(1), 73-85.

DeCaria, Concetta M., Hollander, Eric, Grossman, Robert, Wong, Cheryl M., Mosovich, Serge A., & Cherkasky, Scott (1996). Diagnosis, neurobiology, and treatment of pathological gambling. *Journal of Clinical Psychiatry 57* (supp. 8), 80-84.

Diagnostic and Statistical Manual of Mental Disorders DSM-IV, 4th ed. (1994). Pathological gambling. American Psychiatric Association. pp. 615-618.

Dickerson, Mark (1987, Winter). The future of gambling research learning from the lessons of alcoholism. *Journal of Gambling Behavior 3*(4), 248-255.

Dickerson, Mark (1993). *Internal and external determinants of persistent gambling: problems in generalizing from one form of gambling to another.* Publications of the Gambling Studies Series of the University of Nevada Press.

Dickey, Fred (2000, Jan. 9). California's big gamble. *The Los Angeles Times Magazine* pp. 14-18.

Dixon, Mark R., Hayes, Linda J., & Ebbs, Ralph E. (1998, Sept.). Engaging in "illusory control" during repeated risk taking. *Psychological Reports 83*, 959962.

Downing, Kathryn M., Parks, Michael, & Clayton, Janet (2000, Feb. 25). No to gambling explosion. *The Los Angeles Times:* Editorial.

Dube, Dominique, Freeston, Mark H., & Ladouceur, Robert (1996, Winter). Potential and probable pathological gamblers: where do the differences lie? *Journal of Gambling Studies 12*(4), 419-429.

Dunn, Ashley (2000, May 12). Hooked on games online. *The Los Angeles Times* sec. one.

Eadington, William R. (1987, Summer). Credit play and casinos: profitability, legitimacy, and social responsibility. *Journal of Gambling Behavior 3*(2), 8397.

Eadington, William R. (1987, Winter). Economic perceptions of gambling behavior. *Journal of Gambling Behavior 3*(4), 264-275.

Eadington, William R. (1995, Spring). Preface gambling: philosophy and policy. *Journal of Gambling Studies 11*(1), 9-13.

Eadington, William R., & Cornelius, J. (1993). Gambling behavior and problem gambling. Publication of the Gambling Studies Series of the University of Nevada Press.

Emerson, Michael O., & Laundergan, Clark J. (1996, Fall). Gambling and problem gambling among adult Minnesotans: changes 1990 to 1994. *Journal of Gambling Studies 12*(3), 291-303.

Estes, K., and Brubaker, M. (1994). *Deadly odds, recovery from compulsive gambling.* Simon and Schuster.

Ethical standards of psychologists (1974). American Psychological Association, Inc.

Fessler, Jennifer L. (1996) *Gambling Away the Golden Years.* Wisconsin Medical Journal.

Fisher, Sue, & Griffiths, Mark (1995, Fall). Current trends in slot machine gambling: research and policy issues. *Journal of Gambling Studies 11*(3), 239-247.

Frank, Michael L., & Lester, David (1991, Fall). Suicidal behavior among members of gamblers anonymous. *Journal of Gambling Studies 7*(3), 249-253.

Franklin, Joanna, & Ciarrocchi, Joseph (1987, Spring). The team approach: developing an experimental knowledge base for the treatment of the pathological gambler. *Journal of Gambling Behavior 3*(1), 60-67.

Glazer, Amy (1998, Summer). Pathological gambling. *The Nurse Practitioner 23*(9), 74-81.

Gold, M., & Ferrell. D. (1998, Dec. 13-15). Going for broke. *The Los Angeles Times.*

Goldstein, David (1997, August 20). Gambling opponents urge commission to regulate industry. *Knight-Ridder/Tribune News Service* page 820: K1748.

Goodall, Leonard E. (1994, Winter). Market behavior of gaming stocks: an analysis of the first twenty years. *Journal of Gambling Studies 10*(4), 323-337.

Gorman, Tom, & Morain, Dan (2000, February 17). Vote could transform state's gambling patterns. *The Los Angeles Times,* pp. 1, 32.

Gorman, Tom, & Morain, Dan (2000, February 28). Gaming profits stir fights over tribal membership. *The Los Angeles Times,* pp. A1, A17.

Govoni, Richard, Rupsich, Nicholas, & Frisch, Ron G. (1996, Fall). Gambling behavior of adolescent gamblers. *Journal of Gambling Studies 12*(3), 305317.

Gowen, W. (1986). *Early signs of compulsive gambling.* Hazelden Publications.

Graham, John R., & Lowenfield, Beverly H. (1986, Spring/Summer). Personality dimensions of the pathological gambler. *Journal of Gambling Behavior 2*(1), 58-67.

Gray, James D. (1993). *The dynamics of shame-based addiction.* Publications of the Gambling Studies Series of the University of Nevada Press.

Green, William (1998, April 6). An antidote to credit cards? (drug therapies for compulsive spending, addictive gambling and kleptomania). *Forbes 161*(7), 161 (1).

Griffiths, Mark (1990, Spring). The cognitive psychology of gambling. *Journal of Gambling Studies 6*(1), 31-33.

Griffiths, Mark (1996, Winter). Gambling on the Internet: a brief note. *Journal of Gambling Studies 12*(4), 471-473.

Gupta, Rina, & Derevensky, Jeffery L. (1996, Winter). The relationship between gambling and video-game playing behavior in children and adolescents. *Journal of Gambling Studies 4*, 375-393.

Heineman, Mary (1987, Spring). A comparison: the treatment of wives of alcoholics with the treatment of wives of pathological gamblers. *Journal of Gambling Behavior 3*(1), 27-40.

Heineman, Mary (1988). *Sharing Recovery, Overcoming Roadblocks.* Hazelden Publications.

Heineman, Mary (1989, Winter). Parents of male compulsive gamblers: clinical issues/treatment approaches. *Journal of Gambling Behavior 5*(4), 321-333.

Heineman, Mary (1992). *Losing your shirt.* Compcare Publishers.

Heineman, Mary (1993). *When someone you love gambles.* Hazelden Publications.

Heineman, Mary (1993). *Compulsive gambling: structured family intervention.* Publications of the Gamblers Studies Series of the University of Nevada Press.

Heineman, Mary (1994, Spring). Compulsive gambling: structural family intervention. *Journal of Gambling Studies 10*(1), 67-76.

Hirshey, Gerrie (1994, July 17). Gambling nation. *New York Times Magazine* sec. 6.

Holtgraves, Thomas M. (1988, Summer). Gambling as self-presentation. *Journal of Gambling Behavior 4*(2), 71-77.

Hornblower, Margot (1996, April 1). No Dice: the backlash against gambling. (resisting gaming initiatives in the states). *Time 147*(14), 28 (6).

Hraba, Joseph, & Lee, Gang (1995, Summer). Problem gambling and policy advice: the mutability and relative effects of structural, associational and attitudinal variables. *Journal of Gambling Studies 11*(2), 105-121.

Hraba, Joseph, & Lee, Gang (1996, Spring). Gender, gambling and problem gambling. *Journal of Gambling Studies 12*(1), 83-101.

Hraba, Joseph, Mok, William P., & Huff, David (1990, Winter). Lottery play and problem gambling. *Journal of Gambling Studies 6*(4), 355377.

Hraba, Joseph, Mok, William P., & Huff, David (1991). Tonight's numbers are . . . lottery play and problem gambling. *Journal of Gambling Studies 6,* 355-378.

Hudak, Clark J., Varghese, Rajo, & Politzer, Robert M. (1989, Fall). Family, marital, and occupational satisfaction for recovering pathological gamblers. *Journal of Gambling Behavior 5*(3), 201209.

Jackson, Barry (1996, January 26). Inside a meeting of Gambler's Anonymous, men seek help for betting problem. *Knight-Ridder/Tribune News Service,* p. 126: K2843.

Jacobi, Marianne (1996, Feb. 1). The gambling epidemic: how it is destroying both young and old. *Family Circle 109*(2), 78 (3).

Jacobs, Durand F. (1986, Spring/Summer). A General theory of addictions: a new theoretical model. *Journal of Gambling Behavior 2*(1), 15-31.

Jacobs, Durand F. (1989). *Evidence supporting a general theory of addiction.* Lexington Books.

Jacobs, Durand F. (1989). A review of juvenile gambling in the United States. *Compulsive Gambling: Theory, Research and Practice.* Lexington Books.

Jacobs, Durand F. (1989, February 20). A general theory of addiction. *Behavior Today 20*(8).

Jones, Tamara (1996, November). Gambling their lives away. (women addicted to gambling: includes warning signs of a gambling problem). *Ladies Home Journal 113*(11), 162 (3).

Kaplan, Roy H. (1987, Fall). Lottery winners: the myth and reality. *Journal of Gambling Behavior 3*(3), 168-178.

Kaplan, Roy H. (1990, Winter). Lottery mania: an editor's view. *Journal of Gambling Studies 6*(4), 289-296.

Kaplan, Roy H. (1988, Fall). Gambling among lottery winners: before and after the big score. *Journal of Gambling Behavior 4*(3), 171181.

Kassinove, Jeffery I. (1998). Development of the gambling attitude scales: preliminary findings. *Journal of Clinical Psychology 54*(6), 763-771.

Keslinger Washington Editors, Inc. (1999, September). Coming: a 12-step plan for computer addicts? *Kiplinger's Personal Finance Magazine 53*(9), 23-25.

Kezwer, Gil (1995, January 1). Physicians say government-approved love affair with gambling sure bet to cause problems. *Canadian Medical Association Journal 154*(1), 84-88.

Kramer, Dee (1997, July 1). "Ask the gambling question," FPS told a "secret" addiction becomes more common. *Canadian Medical Association Journal 157*(1), 61-62.

Kuley, Nadia B., & Jacobs, Durand F. (1988, Fall). The relationship between dissociative-like experiences and sensation seeking among social and problem gamblers. *Journal of Gambling Behavior 4*(3), 197-207.

Ladouceur, Robert (1993). Causes of pathological gambling. Publications of the Gambling Studies Series of the University of Nevada Press.

Ladouceur, Robert, Boisvert, Jean-Marie, Pepin, Michel, Loranger, Michael, & Sylvain, Caroline (1994, Winter). Social cost of pathological gambling. *Journal of Gambling Studies 10*(4), 399-409.

Ladoucer, Robert, Sylvain, Caroline, Letarte, Helene, Giroux, Isabella, & Jacques, Christian (1998, March). Cognitive treatment of pathological gamblers. *Behavior Research and Therapy 36*, 11111119.

Lesieur, Henry R. (1988, Spring). Altering the DSM-III criteria for pathological gambling. *Journal of Gambling Behavior 4*(1), 38-47.

Lesieur, Henry R. (1992, May/June). Compulsive gambling. *Transaction Social Science and Modern Society 29*(4).

Lesieur, Henry R. (1993). *Understanding compulsive gambling.* Hazelden Publications.

Lesieur, Henry R. (1993). Female pathological gamblers and crime. Research grant C-000791 New York Office of Mental Health. Publications of the Gamblers Studies Series of the University of Nevada Press.

Lesieur, Henry R. (1994, Winter). Epidemiological surveys of pathological gambling: critique and suggestions for modification. *Journal of Gambling Studies 10*(4), 385-397.

Lesieur, Henry R., and Puig, Kenneth (1987, Summer). Insurance problems and pathological gambling. *Journal of Gambling Behavior 3*(2), 123-135.

Lesieur, Henry R., & Rosenthal, Richard J. (1991, Spring). Pathological gambling: a review of the literature (prepared for the American Psychiatric Association Task Force on DSM-IV Committee on Disorders of Impulse Control Not Elsewhere Classified.) *Journal of Gambling Studies 7*(1), 5-35.

Lester, David (1998, July). Legal gambling and crime. *Psychological Reports 83*, 382.

Levy, Michael, & Feinberg, Marilyn (1991, Spring). Psychopathology and pathological gambling among males: theoretical anc clinical concerns. *Journal of Gambling Studies 7*(1), 41-53.

Lorenz, Valerie C. (1988). *Releasing guilt about gambling.* Hazelden Publications.

Lorenz, Valerie C. (1989, Winter). Some treatment approaches for family members who jeopardize the compulsive gambler's recovery. *Journal of Gambling Behavior 5*(4), 303-311.

Lorenz, Valerie C. (1990, Winter). State lotteries and compulsive gambling. *Journal of Gambling Studies 6*(4), 383-395.

Lorenz, Valerie C. & Yaffee, Robert A., (1986, Spring/Summer). Pathological gambling: psychosomatic, emotional, and marital difficulties as reported by the gambler. *Journal of Gambling Behavior 2*(1), 40-49.

Lorenz, Valerie C. & Yaffee, Robert A., (1988, Spring). Pathological gambling: psychosomatic, emotional, and marital difficulties as reported by the spouse. *Journal of Gambling Behavior 4*(1), 1325.

Lorenz, Valerie C. & Yaffee, Robert A., (1989, Summer). Pathological gamblers and their spouses: problems in interaction. *Journal of Gambling Behavior 5*(2), 113125.

Maurer, Charles D. (1994, Spring). Practical issues and the assessment of pathological gamblers in a private practice setting. *Journal of Gambling Studies 10*(1), 5-19.

McClory, Robert (1992, September/October). The lure of gambling's "easy" money. *Utne Reader.*

McCollum, Cheryl (1996, September). Winning isn't easy. *Wisconsin Medical Journal 96*(9), 614-617.

McCormick, Richard A. (1987, Winter). Pathological gambling: a parsimonious need state model. *Journal of Gambling Behavior 3*(4), 257-263.

McCormick, Richard A. (1994, Spring). The importance of coping skill enhancement in the treatment of the pathological gambler. *Journal of Gambling Studies 10*(1), 77-97.

McCormick, Richard A., & Taber, Julian I. (1991, Summer). Follow-up of male pathological gamblers after treatment: the relationship of intellectual variables to relapse. *Journal of Gambling Studies 7*(2), 99-107.

McElroy, Susan L., Hudson, James I., Pope Jr., Harrison G., Neck Jr., Paul E., Aizley, Harlyn G. (1992, March). The DSM-III-R impulse control disorders not elsewhere classified: clinical characteristics and relationship to other psychiatric disorders. *American Journal of Psychiatry 149*(3), 318-327.

McGraw, R. (1996, Summer). Similarities and differences between chemical and gambling addiction. *Paradigm 1*(3), 12-16.

McGurrin, Martin C. (1992). Pathological gambling: conceptual, diagnostic, and treatment issues. *Practitioners Resource Series.* Sarasota, Florida: Professional Resources Press.

McGurrin, Martin C. & Abt, Vicki (1992, Winter). Overview of public policy and commercial gambling. *Journal of Gambling Studies 8*(4), 325-329.

Mikesell, John L. (1990, Winter). Lotteries in the state fiscal system. *Journal of Gambling Studies 6*(4), 313-329.

Miller, Mary Ann, & Westermeyer, Joseph (1996). Gambling in Minnesota. *American Journal of Psychiatry 153*, 6, 845.

Miller, Michael M. (1996, September). Medical approaches to gambling issues – I: the medical condition. *Wisconsin Medical Journal 96*(9), 623-634.

Miller, Michael M. (1996, September). Medical approaches to gambling issues – II: the medical response. *Wisconsin Medical Journal 96*(9), 635-642.

Miller, Walter (1986, Fall/Winter 1986). Individual outpatient treatment of pathological gambling. *Journal of Gambling Behavior 2*(2), 95107.

Mills, John (1991, Winter). The money laundering control act and proposed amendments: its impact on the casino industry. *Journal of Gambling Studies 7*(4), 301-312.

Mobilia, Pamela (1993, Summer). Gambling as a rational addiction. *Journal of Gambling Studies 9*(2), 121-151.

Mok, William P., & Hraba, Joseph (1991, Winter). Age and gambling behavior: a declining and shifting pattern of participation. *Journal of Gambling Studies 7*(4), 313-333.

Moren, Emanuel (1993). The growing presence of pathological gambling in society: what we know now. Publications of the Gambling Studies Series of the University of Nevada Press.

Ocean, Grant, & Smith, Garry J. (1993, Winter). Social reward, conflict, and commitment: a theoretical model of gambling behavior. *Journal of Gambling Studies 9*(4), 321-339.

Ogintz, Eileen (2000, February 20). Vegas lures with daycare and sights. *The Los Angeles Times* p. L9.

Pasternak, Andrew V. (1997, October 1). Pathological gambling: America's newest addiction? *American Family Physician 56*(5), 1293-1296.

Pathological gambling (1996, January). *Harvard Mental Health Letter.*

Persky, Joseph (1995, Winter). Impact studies, cost-benefit analysis, and casinos. *Journal of Gambling Studies 11*(4), 349-361.

Ravir, Miriam (1993, Spring). Personality characteristics of sexual addicts and pathological gamblers. *Journal of Gambling Studies 9*(1), 17-29.

Reid, R. L. (1986, Spring/Summer). The psychology of the near miss. *Journal of Gambling Behavior 2*(1), 32-39.

Reno, Ronald A. (1996, March-April). The diceman cometh: will gambling be a bad bet for your town? *Policy Review 76*, 40 (6).

Rose, Nelson I. (1988, Winter). Compulsive gambling and the law: from sin to vice to disease. *Journal of Gambling Behavior 4*(4), 240259.

Rose, Nelson I. (1992, Winter). The future of Indian gaming. *Journal of Gambling Studies 8*(4), 383-399.

Rose, Nelson I. (1995, Spring). Gambling and the law: endless fields of dreams. *Journal of Gambling Studies 11*(1), 15-31.

Rosenthal, Richard J. (1986, Fall/Winter). The pathological gambler's system for self-deception. *Journal of Gambling Behavior 2*(2), 108-120.

Rosenthal, Richard J. (1991). *Pathological gambling, proposed DSM-IV criteria.*

Rosenthal, Richard J. (1993). Some causes of pathological gambling. Publications of the Gambling Studies Series of the University of Nevada Press.

Rosenthal, Richard J. (1995, Winter). Communication, the phenomenology of "bad beats": some clinical observations. *Journal of Gambling Studies 11*(4), 367371.

Rosenthal, Richard J., & Lesieur, Henry R. (1992). Self-reported with drawal symptoms and pathological gambling. *American Journal on Addictions 1*(2), 150-154.

Rosenthal, Richard J., & Rugle, Loreen (1994, Spring). A psychodynamic approach to the treatment of pathological gambling: part I. achieving abstinence. *Journal of Gambling Studies 10*(1), 21-41.

Rugle, Loreen J. (1993, Spring). Initial thoughts on viewing pathological gambling from a physiological and intrapsychic structural per spective. *Journal of Gambling Studies 9*(1), 3-15.

Rugle, Loreen J., & Melamed, Lawrence (1993). Neuropsychological assessment of attention deficit disorder in pathological gamblers. *Journal of Nervous and Mental Disease 181*(2), 107112.

Rugle, Loreen J. & Rosenthal, Richard J. (1994, Spring). Transference and countertransference reactions in the psychotherapy of pathological gamblers. *Journal of Gambling Studies 10*(1), 43-65.

Scrimgeour, Gary J. (1993). Problem gambling: any business of a casino? Publications of the Gamblers Studies Series of the University of Nevada Press.

Scriven, Michael (1995, Spring). The philosophical foundation of Las Vegas. *Journal of Gambling Studies 11*(1), 61-75.

Shaffer, Howard J. (1986). *Conceptual crises in the addictions: the role of models in the field of compulsive gambling.* Center for Addiction Studies, Department of Psychiatry, Howard Medical School. Contract #2322905893. Massachusetts Department of Public Health.

Shaffer, Howard J. (1996, Winter). Understanding the means and objects of addiction: technology, the Internet, and gambling. *Journal of Gambling Studies 12*(4), 461-469.

Shaffer, Howard J., & Gambino, Blase (1989, Fall). The epistemology of "addictive disease": gambling as predicament. *Journal of Gambling Behavior 5*(3), 211229.

Shaffer, Howard J. & Gambino, Blase (1993, Summer). Communication, on the epistemology of disease: a response to Walker. *Journal of Gambling Studies 9*(2), 191-195.

Snyder, Robert J. (1986, Spring/Summer). Gambling swindles and victims. *Journal of Gambling Behavior 2*(1), 50-57.

Specker, Sheila M., Carlson, Gregory A., Edmonson, Karen M., Johnson, Paula E., & Marcotte, Michael (1996, Spring). Psychopathology in pathological gamblers seeking treatment. *Journal of Gambling Studies 12*(1), 67-81.

Spunt, Barry, Dupont, Ida, Lesieur, Henry, Liberty, Hillary James, & Hunt, Dana (1998). Pathological gambling and substance misuse: a review of the literature. *Substance Use and Misuse 33*(13), 2535-2560.

Steel, Zachary, & Blasyczynski, Alex (1998). Impulsivity, personality disorders, and pathological gambling severity. *Addiction 93*(6), 895-905.

Steffgen, K. (1995, December). Check compulsive gamblers for attention deficit symptoms. *The Addiction Letter.*

Stein, Sharon A. (1993). *The role of support in recovery from compulsive gambling.* Massachusetts Department of Public Health. Contract #2322905893. Massachusetts Council on Compulsive Gambling.

Steinberg, Marvin A. (1993, Summer). Couples treatment issues for recovering male compulsive gamblers and their partners. *Journal of Gambling Studies 9*(2), 153167.

Steinberg, Marvin A. (1993). Pathological gambling and couple relationship issues. *Journal of Gambling Studies.*

Steinberg, Marvin A. (1997, December). Data point to need for providers to explore gambling issues. *Alcohol and Drug Abuse Week.*

Stinchfield, Randy (1998, August 24). Gambling rates higher among youths than adults. *Alcoholism and Drug Abuse Weekly 10*(33), 8 (1).

Stoil, M. (1994, July-August). Gambling addiction: the nation's dirty little secret. *Behavioral Health Management.*

Strachan, Mary Lou, & Custer, Robert L. (1993). Female compulsive gamblers in Las Vegas. Publications of the Gambling Studies Series of the University of Nevada Press.

Suck, Won Kim (1998, April). APD antagonists in the treatment of impulse control disorders. *Journal of Clinical Psychiatry 59*(4), 159-164.

Taber, Julian I. (1987, Winter). Compulsive gambling: an examination of relevant models. *Journal of Gambling Behavior 3*(4), 219-223.

Taber, Julian I. (1993). Addictive behavior: an informal clinical view. Publications of the Gambling Studies of the University of Nevada Press.

Taber, Julian I., & Chaplin, Martin P. (1988, Fall). Group psychotherapy with pathological gamblers. *Journal of Gambling Behavior 4*(3), 183-195.

Taber, Julian I., Russo, Angel M., Adkins, Bonnie J., & McCormick, Richard A. (1986, Fall/Winter 1986). Ego strength and achieve ment motivation in pathological gamblers. *Journal of Gambling Behavior 2*(2), 69-79.

Tasman, A., Kay, J., & Lieberman, J. (1997). *Psychiatry Volume 2,* 1264-1271. Harcourt Brace and Company.

Templer, Donald I., Moten, Jackie, & Kaiser, George (1994, Fall). Casino gaming offense inmates: what are these men like? *Journal of Gambling Studies 10*(3), 237-245.

Tessler, Jennifer L. (1996, September). Gambling away the golden years. *Wisconsin Medical Journal 96*(9), 618-621.

Tessler, Jennifer L. (1996, September). Physicians' health: getting the help you May need. *Wisconsin Medical Journal 96*(9), 619-621.

Thompson, William (1996, Winter). Communication, the last resort revisited: a comment on changes in America. *Journal of Gambling Studies 11*(4), 373378.

Viets, Lopez V. C., & Miller, W. R. (1997, November). Treatment approaches for pathological gamblers. *Clinical Psychological Review 17*(7), 689-702.

Vitaro, F., Arseneault, L., & Tremblay, R.E. (1997, December). Dispositional predictors of problem gambling in male adolescents. *American Journal of Psychiatry 154*(12), 1769 (2).

Volberg, Rachel A. (1993). *Estimating the prevalence of pathological gambling in the United States.* (Research Grant MH-44295). Violence and Traumatic Stress Research Branch of the National Institute of Mental Health.

Volberg, Rachel A. (1996, Summer). Prevalence studies of problem gambling in the United States. *Journal of Gambling Studies 12*(2), 111-127.

Volberg, Rachel A., & Banks, Steven M. (1990, Summer). A review of two measures of pathological gambling in the United States. *Journal of Gambling Studies 6*(2), 153-163.

Volberg, Rachel A. & Steadman, Henry J. (1992, Winter). Accurately depicting pathological gamblers: policy and treatment implications. *Journal of Gambling Studies 8*(4), 401-411.

Volberg, Rachel A., Dickerson, Mark G., Ladouceur, Robert, & Abbot, Max W. (1996, Summer). Prevalence studies and the development of services for problem gamblers and their families. *Journal of Gambling Studies 12*(2), 215-231.

Walker, Michael B. (1989). Some problems with the concept of "gambling addiction": should theories of addiction be generalized to include excessive gambling? *Journal of Gambling Behavior 5*(3), 179-199.

Walker, Michael B. (1993). Treatment strategies for problem gambling: a review of effectiveness. Publications of the Gambler's Studies Series of the University of Nevada Press.

Walters, Glenn D. (1994, Summer). The gambling lifestyle: I. Theory. *Journal of Gambling Studies 10*(2), 159-181.

Walters, Glenn D. (1994, Fall). The gambling lifestyle: II. Treatment. *Journal of Gambling Studies 10*(3), 219-235.

Wexler, A., & Wexler, S., *Facts on Compulsive Gambling and Addiction.* Resource Center and Clearing House: Center of Alcohol Studies: Rutgers University.

When the wheels won't stop. (Statistics show that compulsive gambling is becoming a problem for a growing number of Americans.)(1997, Dec. 13). *The Economist 345*(8047), 22 (1).

Whitman-Raymond, Robert G. (1988, Summer). Pathological gambling as a defense against loss. *Journal of Gambling Behavior 4*(2), 99109.

Wildman, II, Robert W. (1989, Winter). Pathological gambling: marital-familial factors, implications, and treatments. *Journal of Gambling Behavior 5*(4), 293-301.

Wolfgang, Ann K. (1988, Summer). Gambling as a function of gender and sensation seeking. *Journal of Gambling Behavior 4*(2), 71-77.

You bet your life!: America's gambling binge draws sharp criticism. (March 11) *Current Events 95*(21), 2.

Zion, Maxene M., Tracy, Elizabeth, & Abell, Neil (1991, Summer). Examining the relationship between spousal involvement in gam-anon and relapse behaviors in pathological gamblers. *Journal of Gambling Studies 7*(2), 117-131.

Printed in the United States
212150BV00002B/2/A

9 781934 248102